# WOLVES
## IN PICTURES

**by David Instone**

**In Association With The Birmingham Post & Mail**

**Thomas Publications**

First published in Great Britain in August 2007 by
Thomas Publications, PO Box 17, Newport,
Shropshire, England, TF10 7WT
www.thomaspublications.co.uk

ISBN 978-0-9550585-2-3

Printed and bound by Cromwell Press, Trowbridge

# Contents

# Introduction

Three League Championships, two FA Cups, a couple of League Cups and the Sherpa Van Trophy... the post-war history of Wolverhampton Wanderers is rich indeed. Throw in the goal-filled journey to a major European final, countless nights of combat against the Continent's biggest clubs and even the brush with extinction in the early and mid-1980s and the story becomes more compelling still.

So much trophy-gathering, so many joyous days out at Wembley. And so many personalities. Even starting in 1947 for the purposes of this publication, we have been able to home in on the likes of Cullis, Wright, Williams, Broadbent, Slater, Flowers, Hancocks, Mullen, Wilshaw, Deeley, Clamp, Thomson, Hughes, Richards and Bull - England internationals all while playing their club football at Molineux.

There are others who have been recognised by their countries and many more who haven't been. But it's pertinent in this summer of 2007 to pinpoint from the distinguished cast of these 192 pages one Alexander Derek Dougan. This book had been virtually put to bed when news broke of the proud Ulsterman's sad passing in June, by which time we had already discovered that he must be one of the most photographed players in Wolves' long history. Almost 45 photos of him appear inside but thank goodness we had the opportunity, just, to revisit some of those pages and dress them up as a tribute to a player who, from 1967 to 1975, truly was a fans' favourite.

We believe *Wolves In Pictures* is the biggest, best and most exclusive collection of Wolverhampton Wanderers photos ever published. Well over 400 of them are captured here and, with more than 125 goals or post-goal celebrations among them, we feel sure many memories will be stirred.

It's pure unashamed nostalgia but, even amid all those well-known highlights in the Wolves story, we have worked hard to avoid duplication of images from the many worthy previous books on the club. We have done all we can to ensure that supporters will be poring over the pages and feasting their eyes on hundreds of photos they haven't previously seen - because not one of them, to the best of our knowledge, has been used in any previous Wolves book.

Our partners in this project are the Birmingham Post & Mail and how pleased we are that they have sidestepped the irksome habit some other newspapers have adopted of throwing away old stock. Their picture library is a rare treasure trove and we trust many of our customers, as well as theirs, will join us in thanking them for respecting historic photographs by archiving them, not binning them.

Material has been sourced by us over numerous visits to their Colmore Row offices in Birmingham but we couldn't have seen through this project without the generous assistance of our friends there, nor without the expertise of the various photographers on the Evening Mail, Birmingham Post, Sunday Mercury and Sports Argus whose work makes up the bulk of the content you are about to enjoy. Happy, sad, quirky.....there should be something here for Wolves supporters of all ages.

We would like to say a particular thank-you to Adam Fradgley, from the Post & Mail photographic department. He's a man constantly at the eye of the storm in the company's day-to-day news-gathering operation but has always been enthusiastic and willing in helping bring to fruition an idea that we first mooted with him around four years ago. His encouragement and cooperation are much appreciated, as is his help in locating pictures from the electronic era of the last decade and a bit; the beginning of the end of hard-copy, tangible black and white pictures, sub-editors' markings and all!

The efforts of the Post & Mail's scanning department are also gratefully acknowledged, as is the assistance of the library staff whose job it is to keep good order in an Aladdin's Cave of a football archive. The Evening Mail and Wolves themselves have also generously promoted the book in their columns and other media outlets and so helped many supporters to have their names in the scroll of honour at the back for posterity.

The newspaper world is a tight-knit community and much help has been forthcoming along the way in the loaning of pictures by the Daily Mirror, Huddersfield Examiner, Southampton Daily Echo, Associated Newspapers, Carlisle Evening News, Coventry Telegraph, Pete's Picture Palace, Liverpool Post & Echo, Derby Evening Telegraph, Yorkshire Evening Post, Nottingham Evening Post, Bolton Evening News and Ipswich Evening Star.

Steve Gordos, author of the excellent 2007 tribute to his hero Peter Broadbent (published by Breedon Books), has kindly done the proof-reading in double-quick time and reminded the **_Wolves In Pictures_** author that his grasp of the English language - and Molineux history for that matter - isn't quite everything he thought it was. Dave Bagnall, now a busy freelance photographer, has kindly supplied the colour photography for the front and back, the cover has been expertly designed by Tricia Mills while the author's wife, Liz, has again played a big part on the technical and marketing side in bringing the project to a conclusion.

A picture, we are told, says more than a thousand words, and there are around 27,000 words in this book in the form of captions. So that all adds up to the equivalent of millions of words in this journey through the last 60 years in the life of one of English football's most famous institutions. That total is barely enough but it will do for a start in unlocking a few fond memories....

# POST-WAR GREATNESS

# Post-War Greatness

The final curtain…..Stan Cullis, Molineux captain since the age of 18, leads Wolves out for the last time in the dramatic climax to the 1946-47 title race. On a boiling afternoon on the last day of May, Cullis announced his decision to retire because of continuing problems from a head injury. And he would have ended with a League Championship medal had Wolves even drawn this home game against Liverpool, but the Merseysiders overcame a goal by Scouser Jimmy Dunn in front of more than 50,000 to win, the decider coming when Albert Stubbins escaped from Cullis' marking on a long run. "I could have brought him down but I didn't want to go down in history as the man who decided the title race with a professional foul," Cullis said. Wolves eventually finished third in the table with Manchester United second. Behind Cullis as the players emerge from the tunnel are Billy Crook and Angus McLean.

The proudest of days for Dennis Wilshaw (front row, far right). The Potteries-born forward made his Wolves debut in this home game against Newcastle on March 12, 1949, and rattled in a match-winning second-half hat-trick from the left wing! He was nevertheless left out by Stan Cullis for the next game but still scored seven more goals that season. Pictured are (back row, from left): Lol Kelly, Roy Pritchard, Bert Williams, Bill Shorthouse, Billy Crook. Front row: Leslie Smith, Jimmy Dunn, Jesse Pye, Billy Wright, Sammy Smyth, Dennis Wilshaw.

Wolves take another stride towards winning the FA Cup for the first time in 41 years as the mainly hidden Jesse Pye makes it 2-0 in the final against Leicester on April 30, 1949. Stan Cullis' side beat Chesterfield, Sheffield United, Liverpool, Albion and Manchester United on their way to Wembley, where they were pulled back to 2-1, only for the also-pictured Sammy Smyth to make sure with a magnificent solo goal.

Left: Not a bad three-halfpence worth! Coverage of the Birmingham v Villa top-flight clash at St Andrew's is relegated to secondary status as the front page of the Sports Argus displays news of Wolves' Wembley victory over Leicester. The win went a long way towards making up for the shock and disappointment at the club's defeat against Portsmouth at the same venue ten years earlier in the last pre-war FA Cup final.

Below left: Celebration time for Jesse Pye as he uses the silverware to quench his thirst following his two-goal contribution. The Yorkshire-born forward played once for England - in Wolves' FA Cup winning year - and scored 95 goals in 209 competitive games for the club from 1946 to 1952, netting four times in the triumphant run that ended the long wait for a major prize at Molineux.

Above: Roy Swinbourne risks getting clattered by keeper Johnny Mapson in this quarter-final FA Cup draw at Sunderland on February 24, 1951. Jimmy Dunn (left) and scorer Johnny Walker are also close at hand in a tie that finished 1-1 before Wolves prevailed in the replay 3-1, all three of these pictured players scoring. In the semis, Stan Cullis' side suffered a controversial defeat at the hands of Newcastle.

Left: Bert Williams, from Bradley, Bilston, was an automatic choice in the Wolves goal for well over a decade up to 1957 and was supremely fit. A fanatical trainer, he even donned his match-day kit to show off his devotion here.

Action from Wolves' 0-0 draw at Manchester City on the first day of 1951-52. Above: Billy Wright, Bill Baxter and (hands on hips) Jesse Pye look on as Bill Shorthouse clears from ex-Molineux hero Dennis Westcott, who had returned to his native north after a Wolves career of 124 goals in 144 competitive games. Below: Pye and Jimmy Dunn remain grounded while City keeper Bert Trautmann punches away. Wolves went back to Maine Road in January, 1952, and drew 2-2 in an FA Cup third-round tie before winning the replay 4-1.

Left: All-out effort from Peter Broadbent but it's not enough to get him to this through ball ahead of goalkeeper Stan Hanson in Wolves' home League match against Bolton on August 25 in 1952. The gifted inside-forward was nevertheless on the mark along with the two-goal Roy Swinbourne in a 3-1 win that kept up Wolves' 100 per cent start to the season. In the distance is Johnny Hancocks.

Above: Wolves, who had hammered Arsenal 6-1 in their first League fixture following World War Two, played some stirring games against the Gunners in the late 1940s and early 1950s. Jimmy Mullen is supported by Sammy Smyth here as he drills in a centre from the left at Highbury despite the attentions of home duo Walley Barnes and Alex Forbes.

Above: Roy Swinbourne's flat out and (right) Dennis Wilshaw is in the net as a Wolves raid ends with the ball safely in the hands of keeper Bill Robertson in the game at Chelsea late in September, 1952. Wolves won 2-1 - their second win in a row at the venue - as Les Smith and Wilshaw scored in front of 63,781.

Left: A stumble in Wolves' drive towards their famous first League title triumph in the winter of 1953-54. Billy Wright trails back but neither he, John Short nor keeper Bert Williams can stop the ball bouncing in for one of the two goals by which Arsenal won at Molineux on January 16. Wolves also lost two of their next three games.

# Champions Of England

Action (above and below) from Wolves' last but one game of 1953-54 on a tense Easter Tuesday. Having beaten Huddersfield at Molineux the day before, Stan Cullis' men surprisingly slipped to a 2-1 defeat despite Dennis Wilshaw's goal. A 2-0 home win over Tottenham four days later nevertheless made Wolves champions for the first time - at Albion's expense no less!

No luck here for Dennis Wilshaw, although it wasn't a costly miss as Wolves overpowered Manchester United 4-2 on October 2, 1954. The champions had also put four past Albion at Molineux a few days earlier in a drawn Charity Shield classic and this win - built on goals by Johnny Hancocks (2), Peter Broadbent and Roy Swinbourne - set them off on a run of nine League games without defeat.

Bert Williams races out to deny boyhood Wolves fan Johnny Nicholls in the 1-1 draw with Albion at The Hawthorns on the opening day of the 1955-56 season. The Wanderers' title defence a few months earlier had been a thrilling one, ending with a final placing of second behind Chelsea. Pictured in support of their keeper are two other England stars, Ron Flowers and Billy Wright. Roy Swinbourne scored the visitors' goal and netted 17 times in 14 games before suffering the cruel knee injury that ended his career prematurely.

Wolves' home game with Luton in August, 1956, is remembered as one of the most famous matches of their halcyon years, a 5-4 home victory providing breathtaking entertainment for a 46,000 crowd. Here, Peter Broadbent slips the ball past keeper Bernard Streten to put Wolves in front, Jimmy Murray (2), Bill Slater and Jimmy Mullen scoring the other goals for a side who were two down in ten minutes and then 5-3 up at half-time. Wolves had lost 1-0 at Kenilworth Road only a week before.

# CHAMPIONS OF ENGLAND

Wolves players pose indoors for a change for a team picture taken beneath Molineux's old stand in the 1956-57 season. Back row, from left: Jimmy Murray, Eddie Clamp, George Showell, Noel Dwyer, Joe Gardiner (trainer), Bert Williams, Ron Flowers, Eddie Stuart, Bill Slater. Middle: Stan Cullis (manager), Harry Hooper, Peter Broadbent, Roy Swinbourne, Billy Wright, Bill Shorthouse, Jack Howley (secretary). Front: Norman Deeley, Colin Booth, Ron Howells, Johnny Hancocks, Jimmy Mullen.

Colin Booth receives a £750 benefit cheque from Wolves chairman James Baker in 1956, watched by manager Stan Cullis and (second from left) Molineux vice-chairman Arthur Oakley. Booth, an inside-forward, appeared 82 times for the club and scored 27 goals, helping in the successive League Championship triumphs in 1958 and 1959 before moving to Nottingham Forest in the 1959-60 season.

Malcolm Finlayson clears with difficulty during Wolves' 3-0 defeat at Manchester United on November 3, 1956. The keeper was having his first run in the senior side at a time when results were up and down, big victories over Portsmouth (6-0) and Arsenal (5-2) interspersed among setbacks such as this. Gerry Harris is the leaping defender while Bill Slater, Eddie Stuart and United's Bobby Charlton look on.

Bill Slater, for several seasons an amateur player and a part-timer long after he made the switch to the professional ranks, finds himself in the money as he receives a £750 benefit cheque from Wolves chairman James Baker in September, 1957. The powerful wing-half, later to switch to centre-half, would play 339 competitive games for the club and 12 for England.

# CHAMPIONS OF ENGLAND

Two distinguished Molineux figures at work as Wolves manager Stan Cullis and secretary Jack Howley attend to office matters in March, 1958 - a time when the club were closing in on winning the Championship for the second time. Cullis was at Wolves for 30 years and Howley for more than 45, the latter having arrived as an office boy and been made secretary in 1948.

Below: Ron Flowers slides across to superbly dispossess Jimmy Greaves in the 2-1 win at home to Chelsea on October 19, 1957. In the background is Wolves defender Gwyn Jones. Norman Deeley and Dennis Wilshaw scored for Stan Cullis' men against the side who had pipped them to the 1954-55 Championship, Wolves taking their unbeaten League run to 18 matches before losing to another London club, Tottenham, in front of 58,393 at White Hart Lane on Boxing Day.

Peter Broadbent in action against Newcastle in 1958 - the genial inside-forward missed only two of the League games in Wolves' 1957-58 title-winning season and none of their four Cup ties.

Wolves were mounting a powerful title challenge by the time they overpowered local rivals Birmingham 5-1 in this Molineux clash on February 22, 1958. Even before that month's Munich air disaster, which decimated Manchester United's young squad, Wolves were clear leaders and followed up with six successive First Division victories. Norman Deeley shrugs off Brian Farmer here to open the scoring against Blues and added a second on a day on which Jimmy Murray netted a hat-trick.

Arsenal's Easter Tuesday visit to Molineux proved a blip as far as Wolves were concerned in the 1957-58 title run-in. Having won 2-0 at Highbury the day before, Stan Cullis' side went down 2-1 in the return, with Norman Deeley denied here by Jack Kelsey as defender Jim Fotheringham looks on. Peter Broadbent scored for a side for whom Billy Wright conceded a penalty for the second time in 24 hours.

Job done! Wolves made no mistake in their next home game when they took care of Preston in front of more than 46,000 and so lifted the title for the second time in their history. It was a glorious spring for the club, with the FA Youth Cup also being won in sensational fashion thanks to a Ted Farmer-inspired 6-1 second-leg victory against Chelsea. Acting skipper Eddie Stuart leads the players through all the back-slappers (above), followed by Peter Broadbent and (behind him) Jimmy Murray, who led the marksmen charts with 32 in League and FA Cup. With Billy Wright away on England duty, it was left to Stuart to address the masses by microphone (left) after the victory over runners-up Preston, the trophy actually being handed over by the League president Arthur Drewry at the home second leg of the FA Youth Cup semi-final against Manchester United.

Title winners Wolves subsequently fell just short of equalling Arsenal's all-time record points haul of 66, winning 4-0 at Manchester United on the Monday after beating Preston but then losing 2-1 in their final game - this visit to Sheffield Wednesday. Ron Flowers scored at Hillsborough and tangles here with the home side's Albert Quixall.

The banner says it all at the full-house celebration banquet at Wolverhampton Civic Hall in the spring of 1958. If the club weren't exchanging pleasantries with foreign visitors following high-profile friendlies or toasting the individual successes of their loyal, long-serving players, they were being lauded for winning the English game's top honours.

Right: Billy Wright is wheeled away from training in July, 1958, in a style to which he certainly wasn't accustomed! The high jinks, led by Bill Shorthouse (by then retired as a player and a member of Stan Cullis' backroom), were to celebrate the Wolves and England skipper's wedding to Joy Beverley at a time when Molineux life was very good.

Below: A cabinet full of trophies but all set to go again - Wolves, minus the by-now-retired Bert Williams and Johnny Hancocks, face the camera in August, 1958. Back row, from left: George Showell, Eddie Clamp, Gerry Harris, Joe Gardiner (trainer), Malcolm Finlayson, Jimmy Murray, Bill Slater, Ron Flowers, Eddie Stuart. Front: Bobby Mason, Norman Deeley, Billy Wright, Stan Cullis (manager), Peter Broadbent, Colin Booth, Jimmy Mullen, Jackie Henderson.

Call-up time for Ron Flowers, Billy Wright and Peter Broadbent as they reflect on their latest selection for England in the 1958-59 campaign. Flowers would play 49 times for his country and Broadbent on seven occasions while Wright famously set a mark for others to follow when he took his final tally of caps to 105 before retiring a few months after this summons.

Wolves were still in outstanding form when they travelled to rain-hit Manchester on February 21, 1959, having won six of their previous seven League matches and scored 31 goals. But they were beaten 2-1 by a last-minute Bobby Charlton goal that hoisted United level on points with them at the top. Billy Wright heads clear here in a duel with Dennis Viollett in what proved to be his farewell competitive visit to Old Trafford. Stan Cullis's team, whose goal had come from Bobby Mason, were back up in Manchester a week later and thrashed City 4-1.

# Bye Bye Billy

Virtually the last photo of the great man at his place of work. Billy Wright poses happily for youngster Paul Coudjoe, watched by brother Peter, on the afternoon his playing career finished with the annual colours v whites pre-season game at Molineux early in August of 1959. Wright was due to play for the whites but Stan Cullis switched him at the last minute to protect his record of never having played in the club's reserves.

Johnny Kirkham made his debut and Phil Kelly his home debut as Wolves climbed level on points with leaders Spurs via this win against Manchester United in October, 1959. Eddie Stuart, at centre-half for the first time since the trip to Middlesbrough in 1952, scored an own goal, but Peter Broadbent, pictured here with Munich air crash survivor Bill Foulkes, and Jimmy Murray (2) netted at the other end.

Blackpool goalkeeper Tony Waiters catches Peter Broadbent's hair rather than the ball in Wolves' 1-1 Division One draw at a muddy Molineux on February 6, 1960. Wolves had lost 3-1 away to the Seasiders earlier in the season but rallied and were strongly in the running for a third title running, having rattled in 14 goals in four games at the start of 1960, six of them in their two ties against Newcastle at the start of their FA Cup run.

Magnificent Barcelona reigned supreme in the European Cup round two tie against Wolves in 1959-60, thrashing them 4-0 at the Nou Camp Stadium in front of 80,000 and 5-2 in a return seen by 55,000. They prevailed 9-2 on aggregate despite this scare (left) when, at a free-kick close to the six-yard line, Norman Deeley tried to pinch even more ground! The no 4 seen in animated protest is Garcia and the no 5 is Rodriguez. Below: A fine finish from Sandor Kocsis as he eludes Bill Slater's slide and drives in one of his four goals in the second leg.

Former Wolves keeper Nigel Sims eases the pressure on Aston Villa's goal in the all-West Midlands semi-final of the FA Cup at a packed Hawthorns on March 26, 1960. Jimmy Murray, who would end the campaign with 34 goals after scoring 32 times a couple of seasons earlier, is the Wanderers player closing in on an afternoon on which his saved first-half shot led to the only goal from Norman Deeley. Villa won that season's Second Division title by way of considerable consolation.

# Hail the Wolves! FA Cup winners 1960

The action switches to Wembley as Blackburn keeper Harry Leyland catches safely and so denies Jimmy Murray (left) and Barry Stobart, the youngster who was named in Stan Cullis's line-up at the expense of Bobby Mason after impressing in the previous weekend's 5-1 League victory at Chelsea. Skipper Eddie Stuart was also unlucky not to be playing after losing his regular place to George Showell several weeks earlier. In Blackburn's line-up was Derek Dougan, who had asked for a transfer that very day.

A tale of two goalkeepers…..left: Malcolm Finlayson is in control as he sees a Blackburn effort to safety on his way to his second successive clean sheet in Wolves' joyous FA Cup run. The journey had continued in rounds four, five and six with victories over Charlton, Luton and Leicester respectively, although the impressive Scot missed the latter two through injury and was replaced by Geoff Sidebottom. Below: It's agony for Blackburn's Harry Leyland as Norman Deeley runs away in celebration after turning to shoot home his second goal and Wolves' last in their emphatic 3-0 win. The triumph, in which Footballer of the Year Bill Slater was captain, eased Wolves' disappointment after their narrow failure to pip Burnley to what would have been a third successive League crown.

Home in triumph......and to a heroes' reception. Wolves' coach, bearing the name of Don Everall as usual, inches through the tens of thousands that lined their route from the town's railway station to the Town Hall the day after the Wembley victory over Blackburn in 1960. Skipper Bill Slater (left) and left-back Gerry Harris take their turn here at the front of the bus's open-top platform and show off the silverware as George Showell and Malcolm Finlayson look through the arch.

Ted Farmer made a sensational debut when Wolves, having blooded Gerry Mannion and Barry Stobart in the previous season's corresponding fixture, went to Old Trafford on September 24, 1960. The young forward, pictured below challenging his marker Ronnie Cope and keeper Harry Gregg in the air, scored twice in two minutes just past the half-hour to secure a 3-1 victory for a side who had needed a Des Horne goal to equalise United's early strike. Cope was so unnerved by the runaround he was given that he never played for United's first team again and subsequently joined Luton. Above: Another image from one of no fewer than four wins Wolves recorded at the ground in five seasons as keeper Malcolm Finlayson dives on the ball right on his line to frustrate a young Bobby Charlton. The three defenders are (from left) George Showell, Eddie Stuart and Eddie Clamp.

Above: Bobby Mason drives across a low centre in Wolves' 2-1 League victory at Birmingham in the autumn of 1960. The Tipton-born forward, who scored 54 goals in 173 appearances for the club, netted along with Jimmy Murray in this win, which continued the club's fine record at St Andrew's. It was their fourth success at the ground in four seasons and they won 6-3 and 4-3 in their next two visits, too.

Left: Not just a brilliant footballer! Wolves skipper Bill Slater changes from the famous gold and black to something a little more formal as he leaves Birmingham University after receiving his Bachelor of Science degree - a course he had pursued in his spare time. Lancashire-born Slater had a wonderful career off the field as well and received the OBE in 1982 for services to sport and the CBE a decade and a half later.

Left: The night Wolves' grip on the FA Cup was prised loose. Malcolm Finlayson punches clear but couldn't prevent Second Division Huddersfield from following up a 1-1 draw at Molineux with this 2-1 replay success at Leeds Road in January, 1961. Jimmy Murray's goal was not enough for Wolves, who are also represented in this picture by (from left) Eddie Stuart, Bill Slater and George Showell.

Below left: Malcolm Finlayson is at full stretch as he tries to prevent Scottish giants Rangers causing yet more havoc on their European Cup Winners Cup visit to Molineux on April 19, 1961. Wolves had lost 2-0 at Ibrox Park three weeks earlier in a first leg watched by just under 80,000 but had their moments in this 1-1 draw in the return, particularly when Peter Broadbent scored in what was the club's last tie in Europe for ten and a half years. Finlayson, a Scot, was often close to international honours.

Below: Malcolm Finlayson again in action, this time as he lunges bravely at the feet of Blackpool forward Ray Parry in the 2-2 Division One draw at Molineux in September, 1961. Wolves, having finished third the season before, lost four of their first seven games of 1961-62 despite a brace here by Jimmy Murray. Parry had become the youngest player ever to appear in the First Division when he faced Wolves as a Bolton Wanderers player at the age of 15 years and 267 days in 1951.

# A Gloomier Dawn

The in-rushing Alan Hinton is denied by Albion keeper Ray Potter in this wintry scene from the big Molineux derby on Boxing Day of 1962. The game was abandoned at half-time with Wolves 2-0 up but any thoughts the Baggies had of getting out of jail were scotched when they lost the re-match 7-0 almost three months later, Hinton scoring twice and fellow winger Terry Wharton three times.

Terry Wharton squeezes a left-foot shot round a defender's outstretched leg and beyond the dive of keeper Colin Withers to give Wolves a sixth minute lead on their League visit to Birmingham on March 9, 1963. It was one of 79 goals the right-winger would score in 242 competitive Wanderers games and set up a thrilling 4-3 win in which John Kirkham, Barry Stobart and Peter Broadbent also netted.

Wolves were near the end of the last of their many good seasons under Stan Cullis - many of them magnificent seasons - when Chris Crowe aimed this unsuccessful header at goal (above) in the 2-1 home League win over Fulham on April 27, 1963. Alan Hinton is the other attacker among the visiting trio of (from left) Bobby Keetch, Alan Mullery and George Cohen in a game which helped Wolves towards a final placing of fifth.

Left: A landmark that stood on the Wolverhampton landscape for decades went up in the early 1960s - much to the satisfaction of long-serving Molineux secretary Jack Howley (left). The Wolves Social Club, a magnet for supporters, cost almost £100,000 and was seen as being ahead of its time 45 years ago. The facility stood between the ground and Waterloo Road near two of the car parks that are in use today.

Left: Signing day at Molineux for the Ipswich Town and England centre-forward Ray Crawford on September 16, 1963. Stan Cullis certainly needed him. Wolves had just lost three games in a row and would crash to a spectacular 6-0 defeat at Liverpool on his debut before he started to click with both goals in a 2-1 victory at Blackpool - only the club's third win of a season that was by then nine games old.

Below: Molineux gates were down below 20,000 by the time Wolves contested this 2-2 League draw with the top flight's other Wanderers, Bolton, on October 19, 1963. It was a sure sign the rot was setting in after all the glories of the previous decade and a half - and the slide had a good way still to go to bottom out. Ray Crawford is the man on the ball here as he bursts in between the visiting duo of Roy Hartle (right) and keeper Alex Smith.

Above: All the necessary mod cons for Wolves as they hit the road for an away game in their new Don Everall coach in the autumn of 1963. Chris Crowe is the man at the control of the TV (black and white no doubt!) and (from left) Jimmy Murray, Fred Davies, Alan Hinton and George Showell are the four card-playing members of the squad facing the camera.

Left: Ray Crawford, having made his Wolves debut in a 6-0 defeat at Liverpool, quickly became a lucky omen for the club as they embarked on an undefeated run that stretched to eight matches with this 2-0 home win over Manchester United on November 2, 1963. Crawford and Terry Wharton scored against the FA Cup holders, who are represented here by keeper Harry Gregg and centre-half Bill Foulkes.

Ray Crawford is the main man again here, flicking the ball past goalkeeper Roy Bailey for one of Wolves' goals in their 2-1 home win over his former club Ipswich on November 16, 1963. Stan Cullis' men had lost at Burnley the week before and would suffer heavy subsequent defeats at Sheffield Wednesday and Fulham as their fortunes begin to dip. In front of an attendance of only 17,891 for the visit of the Suffolk side, Peter Broadbent is the home player in the background.

Stan Cullis' transfer-market record was not flawless and this deal didn't help him. Wolves lost Alan Hinton (second left) to Nottingham Forest and signed Dick Le Flem (second right) in exchange, Hinton's career taking off in the East Midlands while Guernsey-bred Le Flem lasted only a year at Molineux. Also pictured are managers Johnny Carey and Cullis and (standing) secretary Jack Howley.

Wolves were lurching towards a disappointing final placing of 16th when they fought out this 1-1 Molineux draw with Blackpool on February 1, 1964. Ray Crawford, denied here by Tony Waiters' dive at his feet while England right-back Jimmy Armfield looks on, scored the home side's goal in the game that marked Dick Le Flem's debut but the 16,345 crowd showed that the club were on the slide.

It's August, 1964, the players are in v-neck shirts and Stan Cullis appears at a pre-season photo-call as Wolverhampton Wanderers manager for the last time. Back row (from left): Johnny Kirkham, Chris Crowe, Dick Le Flem, Peter Broadbent, Fred Davies, Gerry Harris, Dave Woodfield, George Showell, Bobby Woodruff. Middle row: Stan Cullis, Fred Goodwin, Terry Wharton, Ron Flowers, Bobby Thomson, Ray Crawford, Peter Knowles, Joe Gardiner (coach). Front row: Jimmy Melia, Ted Farmer.

# End Of A Golden Age

Wolves started 1964-65 with six defeats out of seven and Stan Cullis' 16-year reign as manager ended in mid-September despite a thrilling 4-3 home victory over West Ham. Previously a majestic England international centre-half, Cullis had been absent from his post for some time through illness but posed for photographs (right) with the letter informing him of his dismissal.

Andy Beattie was the man Wolves turned to as fire-fighter in the autumn of 1964 but the side were still in big relegation danger when (below) they played this FA Cup fourth-round tie against Second Division Rotherham. On a frost-bound surface, Ray Crawford opened the scoring with a fine header pictured here, only for the team to fall 2-1 in arrears before Ron Flowers equalised two minutes from the end. The players are wearing black armbands to commemorate the funeral of Sir Winston Churchill on the same day. The Rotherham no 5 is Peter Madden.

Wolves won 3-0 at Rotherham in their replay shortly before the sale of Ray Crawford to Albion, then needed three games to beat Villa, who they had last met in the FA Cup in the 1960 semi-final. Like then, the tie was settled at The Hawthorns, Hugh McIlmoyle this time hitting a hat-trick. George Miller consoles the losers (above) on a snow-bound pitch, Wolves - experimentally wearing gold shorts - subsequently beating Birmingham, Albion and Stoke in the League but losing 5-3 at home to Manchester United in round five of the Cup.

New division, new season, new coach….Ronnie Allen, recruited to work with Andy Beattie, prepares for training with relegated Wolves in July, 1965. From left are Dave Woodfield, George Miller, Dave MacLaren, Hugh McIlmoyle, Bobby Thomson, Ron Flowers and Fred Davies. Allen was an Albion playing legend who was put in charge of Wolves in September, 1965, when Beattie departed.

Andy Beattie's last act at Molineux was to sign Ernie Hunt for £40,000 from Swindon. The newcomer is pictured with his wife Anne and (far left) his former Swindon team-mate Bobby Woodruff, already on Wolves' playing staff. Hunt didn't play two days later in the 9-3 thrashing at Southampton which was one of Wolves' heaviest all-time defeats - enough to prompt Beattie's departure.

Two spectacular games from the first half of Wolves' programme in the 1965-66 Second Division. Above: It's agony at The Dell as Terry Paine hits Southampton's third goal in their 9-3 slaughter of Andy Beattie's side in the middle of September. Ron Flowers is the man on the line trying to block the shot while the no 2 is Joe Wilson and the grounded goalkeeper is David MacLaren. Surprisingly, Wolves had scored first in one of their heaviest ever defeats.

Left: Hugh McIlmoyle (close to goal) and Terry Wharton wait for a slip by a Portsmouth defence who conceded no fewer than eight goals in this clash at Molineux in late November. Bobby Woodruff, McIlmoyle and central defender John Holsgrove each scored twice for a Wolves team who let in two at the other end.

This 1-0 Wolves victory against Crystal Palace in October, 1965 - a success that left them fourth in the Second Division table - meant they had won five and drawn one of six games following their 9-3 mauling at Southampton. A lob by no 10 Peter Knowles (right) saw off Palace, who included David Burnside in their side and who got changed on the train when it was sufficiently delayed at Leamington as to put the kick-off back to 3.30pm. Dave Woodfield challenges keeper John Jackson here. Bobby Thomson is also pictured.

Joe Wilson (no 2) and John Holsgrove (no 6) watch Dave Woodfield challenge as Wolves defend in their 2-1 defeat at Carlisle in February, 1966. Striker Hugh McIlmoyle was made captain against his old team but the result wasn't a big surprise. Although Carlisle had lost 12 successive away games, they had taken 19 points from 24 at home. Dave Wagstaffe's equaliser briefly lifted Wolves, who followed their first visit to Brunton Park by going to Lytham St Anne's for a pre-FA Cup break.

Two walkers and a furry friend allow Wolves players past on a run on the Lytham St Anne's sands before the club's FA Cup fifth-round tie at home to Manchester United in March, 1966. The Cup was a huge thing in those days, the 4-2 defeat against United attracting a season's best 53,428 to Molineux while the earlier wins over Altrincham and Sheffield United pulled in 30,475 and 32,456 respectively.

So this is Molineux…..Charlton and England midfielder Mike Bailey surveys his new surroundings after being signed by Ronnie Allen for a bargain £40,000 late in the winter of 1965-66. Bailey made his debut in the draw at home to Southampton on March 1 and gave the club magnificent service over more than a decade. He couldn't stop them coming up short in their promotion challenge, though, the side finishing sixth in Division Two in 1965-66 after winning only one of their final four matches.

John Holsgrove (left) and Davy Burnside watch Dave Woodfield clear his lines in Wolves' 3-1 win at Carlisle on September 10, 1966. Ernie Hunt (2) and Holsgrove scored in a game that was notable for marking the start of Mike Bailey's lengthy spell as captain in succession to Bobby Thomson. Three days earlier, Burnside's name appeared in Crystal Palace's line-up in the Molineux programme but he played instead for Wolves and scored in a 1-1 draw after making the move north from Selhurst Park.

Wolves stayed in the goal-scoring habit in a big way with this 7-1 Molineux crushing of Cardiff on September 21, 1966. The Welsh club had lost 9-1 at home to Wolves just over a decade earlier and were no match for them here, Bobby Thomson scoring his first goal for the club and Terry Wharton including this penalty and another spot-kick in his hat-trick. The floundering keeper is Lyn Davies.

Wolves returned to top spot in the Second Division when they completed a high-scoring festive double over Derby in 1966 that set down a marker in the promotion race. Hugh McIlmoyle, who would end his stay at Molineux with the more than useful haul of 45 goals in 105 games, rises powerfully to equalise at 1-1 against the Rams on Christmas Eve in a game Wolves went on to win 5-3 - a success they built on with a 3-0 Boxing Day win at the Baseball Ground. It was in the latter game that McIlmoyle scored his last League goal for the club.

After the goal feast home and away against Derby, there was no way through for Wolves in a frustrating 0-0 draw with Ipswich at Molineux on New Year's Eve, 1966. McIlmoyle was again to the fore as he sought to add to a League goal tally that already stood at 13 for the season. But Wolves were becalmed and scored only once in four Second Division matches as progress suddenly became a little tougher.

# Back To The Big Time

Fans' fashions early 1967 style! Scarves, hats and a rattle or two are all part of the garb for these supporters before Wolves' 1-1 FA Cup fourth-round draw with Everton on February 18. And the youngsters had plenty to cheer. Their side, who beat Oldham in a round-three replay, were in a rich goal-scoring vein with 5-2 and 3-1 League victories over Bolton and Charlton in their previous two matches.

In excess of 113,000 spectators saw the two matches Wolves contested against FA Cup holders Everton in the fourth round in mid-February, 1967. There were 53,439 at Molineux for this draw in which Terry Wharton scored, then 60,020 descended on Goodison Park to see the favourites prevail 3-1 in the replay - despite another goal by Wharton. Bobby Thomson and Jimmy Husband do battle here as Mike Bailey looks on.

It took only one game and probably just one goal for Derek Dougan to become a North Bank hero. Signed shortly before from Leicester, the Northern Ireland international made his debut in a 1-0 win at Plymouth and then played his first home match here against Hull a week later on March 25, 1967. This magnificent goal after he flicked the ball over a defender was the highlight of his hat-trick in a 4-0 victory.

Phil Parkes catches as Second Division leaders Wolves proceed towards an Easter double over Huddersfield in March, 1967. Ronnie Allen's side followed up this 1-0 victory at Leeds Road - secured by Terry Wharton's goal - by prevailing again against the West Yorkshiremen 24 hours later and making it eight wins in a row, the last five without conceding a goal. Full-back Gerry Taylor is the no 2 by the post as Bobby Thomson and John Holsgrove also cover. The home side are in plain shirts as part of a brief experiment that saw them forsaking their usual blue and white stripes.

Happy times for the Molineux squad as they record the 'Hungry Wolves' LP with DJ Jimmy Henney and composer Gordon Franks in April, 1967. The musical interlude was to mark the club's promotion back to the top flight - secured with the 4-1 home victory over Bury.

Wolves won promotion with three games to play - but the title started to slip away in this famous 3-1 defeat at Coventry in front of 51,455. After a Peter Knowles opener, the Sky Blues rallied and Ronnie Rees flashed one of their goals (above) past Graham Hawkins and keeper Phil Parkes on a late April day that ended with a pitch invasion to celebrate Coventry's feat of reaching the top flight for the first time. The no 6 walking off at the end is John Holsgrove.

Left: Saying it with flowers......bouquets were handed to fans as a thank-you at the end of Wolves' 1966-67 promotion campaign. Mike Bailey, who was an ever-present until injury ruled him out of the final game at Crystal Palace, does the honours here before the thumping 4-1 home victory against Norwich in the last of Joe Wilson's 63 Wanderers outings.

Below: A fun time to be at Molineux......Shadows and in particular Hank Marvin fan John Holsgrove leads this 1967 musical session in the company of (left to right) Terry Wharton, Peter Knowles, captain Mike Bailey, Ernie Hunt and Bobby Thomson. There was a lot to sing about with Wolves back in the big time at the second attempt after a season in which Carlisle and Blackburn finished third and fourth respectively, albeit six and seven points behind second spot.

Derek Dougan climbs high to test Crystal Palace's defence in the last game of 1966-67 but Wolves' 4-1 defeat at Selhurst Park meant they missed out on the title. Coventry beat Millwall 3-1 at Highfield Road at the same time to deny a side who had needed only a point to be crowned champions. Ernie Hunt scored Wolves' goal but it was not enough despite the presence in attack of Dave Woodfield here. Ex-Molineux forward Bobby Woodruff scored one of Palace's four - the most Wolves had conceded in a game all season.

Cheers, we're going up! Manager Ronnie Allen pours a drop of the strong stuff for (from left) Davy Burnside, Graham Hawkins, Bobby Thomson and Fred Davies at the civic banquet staged in late May to celebrate Wolves' promotion after two seasons in Division Two. The side had been helped over the line by Derek Dougan, who was signed from Leicester in March and who responded with nine goals.

Wolves hadn't finished for summer when they ended their Division Two season on May 13, 1967. In an undertaking totally unheard of today, they then spent a month and a half playing as Los Angeles Wolves and winning a tournament in the USA. The last of their 14 games was an epic 6-5 victory over an Aberdeen team who included Frank Munro. Pictured with the cup are (left to right) Derek Dougan, manager Ronnie Allen, Bobby Thomson and Dave Woodfield.

Below: A jubilant Derek Dougan opens the scoring with a fine 33rd minute header in Wolves' game at Fulham on the first day of the 1966-67 First Division programme. Just-promoted Wolves, watched at Craven Cottage by Billy Wright, increased the lead through Mike Bailey and held on to win 2-1. Ernie Hunt is the Wolves player on his knees and Tony Macedo is the floundering goalkeeper.

Top-flight life soon proved more difficult for Wolves, who were sliding when despatched from Liverpool on November 25, 1967, on the end of a third successive defeat. Ron Yeats goes close with a header here as Derek Dougan challenges and keeper Evan Williams, John Holsgrove and no 3 Bobby Thomson closely watch the ball's flight. Alun Evans scored Wolves' goal in a 2-1 defeat.

The perfect host....Mike Bailey had taken on a restaurant business in Birmingham after settling in the area and was happy to extend a mid-season invitation across the West Midlands patch to Birmingham skipper Ron Wylie (centre) and Albion defender John Kaye. This early-December visit came in between victories at home to Southampton and Fulham that kept Wolves comfortable in mid-table.

Ronnie Allen proved himself a quite brilliant spotter of players for the Molineux cause, signing Kenny Hibbitt, Derek Dougan, Mike Bailey, Frank Munro and Derek Parkin, among others, at low cost. Full-back Parkin, pictured above with his wife and Allen, arrived from Huddersfield on Valentine's Day, 1968, and has played more first-team Wolves games (609) than any other man in history. Munro, pictured below with the manager, came to Wolves' attention when playing against them for Aberdeen (alias Washington Whips) in the 1967 USA Tournament. He scored a hat-trick in the final of that competition and moved south, initially as a forward, for £55,000 in the following January, becoming a massive favourite for Wolves supporters over the next decade.

Wolves had gone ten games without a win when they held Liverpool 1-1 on March 2, 1968. The club were leaking too many goals for comfort, although John Holsgrove and Derek Parkin, the latter on his home debut, give good cover here as keeper Phil Parkes goes up with no 5 Ron Yeats. In the background on a day when Derek Dougan scored the Wolves goal are Bobby Thomson and Peter Knowles.

All smiles as Mike Bailey receives the Evening Mail Trophy from Wolves chairman John Ireland to mark his winning of the Midlands Footballer of the Year award in the spring of 1968. The skipper and driving midfielder was a colossus of a figure, following up his 41 League appearances out of 42 in the club's promotion season with an identical number the next. Sadly, though, despite one or two near misses, he was unable to add at Molineux to the two England caps he had won as a Charlton player in the mid-1960s.

Two key moments from Wolves' crushing 6-1 win over Nottingham Forest on April 6, 1968 - a result that ended a run of three defeats and boosted their hopes of survival. Below: Derek Dougan drives past keeper Mick Harby for the first goal of his second hat-trick for the club. The visitors had John Barnwell in their ranks but were no match for Wolves, whose ex-Forest striker Frank Wignall climbs above Terry Hennessey (left) to nod one of his two. Hennessey is a distant relative of present-day Wolves and Welsh keeper Wayne Hennessey.

No way through for champions-elect Manchester City as Derek Dougan performs a balancing act while defending at Molineux on April 20, 1968. Almost 40,000 saw Wolves take another step to safety and City inch closer to lifting the League title only two years after winning promotion. George Heslop is the City man and Derek Parkin and Dave Woodfield the defenders keeping an eye on him.

What Derek Dougan had done in 1966-67, Frank Wignall did in 1967-68. Wignall hit nine goals in his first 12 Wanderers games, including this treble at home to Chelsea in the penultimate game of the club's season. Defender Dave Webb is the man getting a rocket from Marvin Hinton, John Hollins preferring to quietly survey the damage. Wignall, signed from Nottingham Forest, then scored twice in a win at home to Spurs as Wolves finished in relative comfort.

Having finished 17th in 1967-68, Wolves were keen to do better when they regrouped in July, ready for the short trip to Cannock Chase for their first day of pre-season training. With a young John McAlle (second right) having made the first of his 508 appearances for the club, they again started slowly, though, with a defeat at newly-promoted Ipswich being followed by another loss at Manchester City.

Bob Wilson, who tried his luck at Wolves as a youngster, punches clear in Arsenal's lively 0-0 draw at Molineux on August 21, 1968. Frank Wignall is the attacker putting the keeper under pressure while John Holsgrove and a more distant Dave Woodfield keep an eye on proceedings. Wolves had opened their points account after two opening defeats by beating QPR 3-1 four days earlier.

Frank Wignall shields the ball from John Talbut in Wolves' 0-0 League draw at Albion on September 21, 1968. The striker had started the season well with four goals but the side had gone four games without a win come the time of this derby, in which their hopes were hit by the early loss of an injured Dave Wagstaffe. Others pictured are John Holsgrove and Albion duo Doug Fraser and Graham Lovett.

Alan Boswell, an eccentric keeper just signed from Shrewsbury, saves at the feet of Tony Hateley as Wolves hit back from their notorious 6-0 home defeat against Liverpool by winning 1-0 at Coventry on October 5, 1968. Ronnie Allen's side clung to their first away win of the season thanks to Derek Dougan's brave header and have John Holsgrove and Dave Woodfield as the covering defenders here.

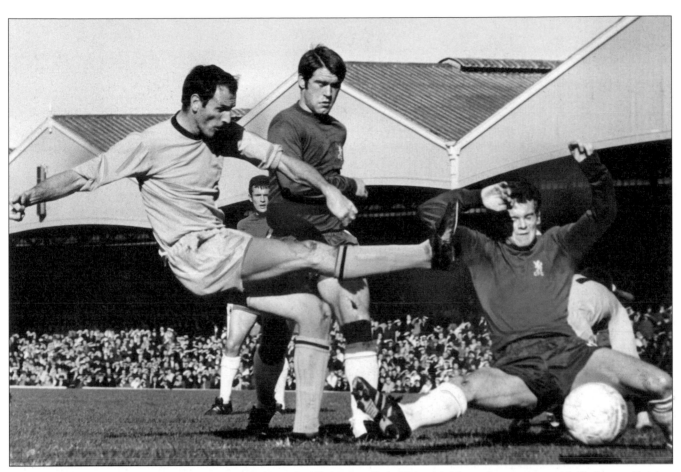

Derek Dougan can't force a way past the outstretched leg of Eddie McCreadie in Wolves' 1-1 home League draw with Chelsea on October 12, 1968. David Webb and John Hollins are the other visiting players in view on a day when Peter Knowles struck the home team's goal. Wolves had won only three of their first 14 Division One games and then lost in the League Cup at Blackpool four days later.

So close for The Doog as this left-foot shot on the run crashes against the post in Wolves' vital 2-0 Molineux success over West Ham on November 9, 1968. Skipper Mike Bailey, pictured in the distance, and right-winger John Farrington scored the goals, both in the last 15 minutes. Bobby Moore is the closest defender for a Hammers side who were the First Division's joint highest scorers at the time.

# Did that *really* happen?

## Strange events in Wolves' long proud history

Above: Which way to the pitch? Terry Wharton might almost be wondering whether he will have to pay to get back in after spilling over among the spectators in Wolves' 2-1 Molineux win over Plymouth on October 22, 1966 - the club's fifth successive League victory at home. The winger, a penalty expert, later joined his home-town club Bolton. Below: Ever the showman, Derek Dougan has a brush with his adoring public in the 3-0 victory over Manchester City on October 24, 1970.

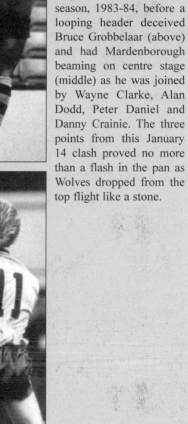

Steve Mardenborough hit only one goal in 11 senior matches for Wolves - and what a memorable one it was! Of all places, it came at Liverpool, who were marching towards lifting the title for the third year running. Wolves had won only three times in that season, 1983-84, before a looping header deceived Bruce Grobbelaar (above) and had Mardenborough beaming on centre stage (middle) as he was joined by Wayne Clarke, Alan Dodd, Peter Daniel and Danny Crainie. The three points from this January 14 clash proved no more than a flash in the pan as Wolves dropped from the top flight like a stone.

Molineux's famous old Waterloo Road Stand was flattened in 1992 to pave the way for the showpiece Billy Wright Stand in the magnificent 'new' ground bankrolled by Sir Jack Hayward. But, on the day of the last game before the arrival of the bulldozers - at home to Middlesbrough - a multitude of incendiary devices were found buried in the pitch. Fortunately, they were spotted in time and safely removed on the morning of the match. The perpetrators were never caught.

# McGarry Rule

Wolves' slow start to 1968-69 cost Ronnie Allen his job and they looked to Ipswich for his replacement. Like Allen, Bill McGarry was Potteries-born and even played in the same Port Vale side. Molineux chairman John Ireland (left) unveiled him in the Midlands towards the end of November, with secretary Jack Howley (centre) also striding out here en route from the car park for the ground's main entrance.

Right, you lot, no slouching! Bill McGarry soon let it be known who was boss at Molineux and had his players lapping the pitch on his first day at the club. From left, Bobby Thomson, John Holsgrove, Derek Clarke, John McAlle, Phil Parkes, Peter Knowles and Dave Wagstaffe are put through their paces, Wolves having thrashed Newcastle 5-0 in their last game before the new manager's arrival.

With Bill McGarry in the crowd but not officially in charge, Wolves thrashed Newcastle 5-0 at Molineux on November 23, 1968. But the manager couldn't have had a tougher baptism than a trip a week later to European Cup holders Manchester United, where his Ipswich side had gained a creditable draw in his final game before he departed from Portman Road. Wolves were not as successful and lost 2-0, George Best (above) shooting the first and the points being sealed by a late header by Denis Law (below), who also sees Phil Parkes take a cross under pressure (bottom picture) as Bobby Thomson, Dave Woodfield, Peter Knowles and Mike Bailey look on.

The different preparations players make before a trip to the seaside…..right: John Holsgrove seems to be convinced he will have every opportunity for some quality strumming time during Wolves' trip to Southport prior to their third-round FA Cup tie at Second Division Hull in the first week of January, 1969. At his side, full-back Bobby Thomson has opted for the footballer's no 1 other pastime - and reached for his golf clubs.

Above: It may be a break from home but there's still a lengthy journey to be made. Whatever may be packed in the hold, Frank Wignall (left), Phil Parkes (centre) and winger John Farrington decide there's no need for anything more extravagant than a game of cards as the team coach is about to depart from Molineux. Wolves prevailed 3-1 at Boothferry Park, Derek Dougan scoring twice and Wignall once.

Wolves' FA Cup run ended at the fourth-round stage when they were beaten 2-1 by Tottenham in front of 48,985 at White Hart Lane on January 25, 1969. Dave Wagstaffe was on target for Bill McGarry's side but they couldn't hold Jimmy Greaves, who is pictured scoring one of Spurs' goals above despite Phil Parkes' dive and the presence on the line of Derek Parkin. No 10 is Les Wilson, with Dave Woodfield the other Wolves player in view. It was a big day for John McAlle, who was making only his second senior start, the first having come at Chelsea. He joins Derek Dougan in attack (below) as Mike England and (left) Alan Gilzean do the marking.

Peter Knowles scored in this 1-1 home League draw against Burnley on February 1, 1969, but most Molineux eyes were on Hugh Curran, pictured here during his debut for the club. The Scottish striker cost £60,000 from Norwich and would pay back that investment by netting 47 times in 98 Wanderers appearances, his first entry on the score-sheet coming a week later in a 2-2 draw at home to European Cup holders Manchester United.

Above: Peter Knowles tussles with Liverpool left-back Gerry Byrne - a member of England's 1966 World Cup party - during Wolves' trip to Anfield on April 5, 1969. Bill McGarry's team lost 1-0 in front of a crowd of more than 45,000.

Peter Knowles gives the slip to Albion left-back Ray Wilson in the derby at Molineux in April, 1969. Wolves had just ended a run of six games without a win by beating Manchester City 3-1 but lost 1-0 to the Baggies and, despite a Knowles goal in the home draw with Coventry three days later, didn't win again that season as they finished 16th in the table. Against Albion, Kenny Hibbitt made his senior debut as substitute, although it was another 18 months before he made his first start.

Offside is the call as Derek Dougan fires goalwards while Southampton keeper Gerry Gurr rushes out in Wolves' second game of the 1969-70 campaign. Wolves conceded an own goal through Derek Parkin but nevertheless won 2-1 to add to their opening-day 3-1 home victory over Stoke and stretch a 100 per cent that would then continue with 3-2 wins at Sheffield Wednesday and in the return clash at Southampton. Ken Jones is the Saints defender captured in mid-appeal. Peter Knowles and Frank Munro were Wolves' marksmen in this game, which marked the switching-on of Molineux's new £20,000-plus floodlights.

It was early in 1969, as Wolves advanced towards a modest 16th-place finish in the top flight, that Peter Knowles started to talk about the beliefs that threatened his football future. With his light blue jaguar in the background, the gifted inside-forward finds himself in the firing line in front of the Wolves Social Club at the hands of reporters keen to learn about his interest in becoming a Jehovah's Witness.

# The Fondest Of Farewells

The news that all Wolves supporters had been dreading came early in 1969-70 when Peter Knowles confirmed he was quitting football to become a full-time Jehovah's Witness. His last appearance in a 191-match Molineux career that brought him no fewer than 64 goals came at home to Nottingham Forest on September 6, when (right) he found himself up against John Barnwell - a man later to serve as Wolves manager. Below: Disappointed fans at least looked like having a victory to toast on the occasion of Knowles' farewell as this bouncing header by Derek Dougan past keeper Alan Hill made it 2-0 and helped Wolves build a three-goal lead. But Bill McGarry was an angry man at the end of the afternoon after his players had been pegged back by three second-half Forest goals before almost losing it in the last minute.

Peter Knowles was never short of admirers, especially female ones, and was a magnet for attention as he said his sad goodbyes (below). At the end of a fixture in which Hugh Curran (right) scored twice for a side who had started the season with four consecutive victories, Knowles did not hang around for handshakes, running quickly for the tunnel and escaping almost all the well-wishers! Showered and dressed, he was later confronted by two young girls who had found their way back into Molineux to enjoy a special audience with the man who was breaking their hearts. But he craved the escape from the spotlight that he found in the photo on the bottom right. In what was the Beatles era, Wolves retained the registration of this crowd idol for several years hoping he'd change his mind. But he never did - and is now in his 60s.

Left: Jim McCalliog, signed in the summer of 1969 and clearly one of Bill McGarry's most successful signings, challenges Peter Bonetti in a 2-2 draw at Chelsea in Wolves' first game after Peter Knowles' retirement. Also closing in on the keeper, who became a coach at Molineux in the 1990s, is Hugh Curran. The latter scored twice for the second Saturday running and would shortly do likewise in a 3-2 third-round League Cup victory at Brighton.

Below: Burnley defend in numbers in their League clash away to Wolves on September 20, 1969. Jim McCalliog (pictured left) equalised for a side for whom Paul Walker had a rare run-out in attack in this fourth successive 1-1 draw between the two sides. Wolves then made two visits to Turf Moor in the following January, losing heavily in the FA Cup third round but winning 3-1 in the League a week later, McCalliog again scoring. Derek Dougan is the man doing the pressing here, flanked by Martin Dobson.

Not this time for Mike O'Grady (left) during Wolves' game against Albion on November 1, 1969, although he had the last say in this Molineux derby. The forward, signed from Leeds a few weeks earlier, is denied here by Graham Williams but found the target with a spectacular late drive in Wolves' 1-0 win in front of the Match of the Day cameras. No 9 Derek Dougan was playing his last game before an astonishing ban of eight weeks.

Below: Bertie Lutton, an Ulsterman little used at Molineux, certainly made his mark in this 2-0 home league victory against Arsenal on November 15, 1969, scoring just after half-time and almost immediately flicking the ball past keeper Geoff Barnett for Hugh Curran to net the killer second. Wolves drew 0-0 at Liverpool seven days earlier.

Hugh Curran beats Jim Montgomery with a 21st minute header to settle Wolves' home clash with Sunderland on November 29, 1969. On a frozen pitch, the striker evades the nearby Colin Todd as Frank Munro (left) - then a forward - follows up to make sure. The game was the first English match shown live on TV in Scandinavia - exposure that gained Wolves considerable support in that part of the world.

Misery followed Wolves all over the City Ground in this pre-Christmas clash in 1969. Dave Wagstaffe hit the bar with an early penalty and Hugh Curran was stretchered off with a back injury on a frost-bound day on which the side hit back from 2-0 down to 2-2, only to lose 4-2 to Nottingham Forest. Phil Parkes, Dave Woodfield and John Holsgrove are powerless here as Dave Hilley opens the scoring.

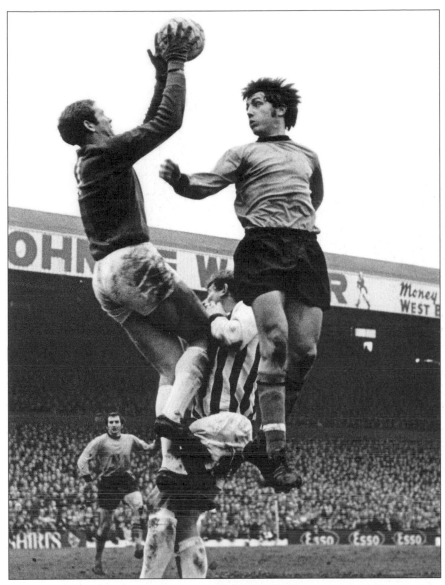

Debut day for John Richards (left) - and what a day! Bill McGarry chose the Black Country derby away to Albion on February 28, 1970, to blood the 19-year-old from Warrington but there was no joy for him here as Jim Cumbes climbed above him and John Kaye. In the distance is Mike O'Grady, who scored one of Wolves' goals in a thrilling 3-3 draw, Hugh Curran netting the other two - one of them from a penalty.

Below: A second senior game at Molineux for John Richards (centre) as he watches a header from Jim McCalliog float towards goal in Wolves' League clash at home to Leeds on March 21, 1970. Bill McGarry's men lost 2-1 despite another of Hugh Curran's 23 goals that season and finished in 13th place - a modest improvement on their previous two years since promotion, although they failed to win any of their last 13 League matches. Leeds were champions at the time and are represented here by Paul Madeley, Terry Yorath and Terry Cooper.

Wolves did battle in the Anglo Italian Cup at the end of 1969-70 and unluckily failed to make progress despite winning three of their four matches. Hugh Curran and Derek Dougan lead the charge (left) in the 2-1 victory at home to Fiorentina in front of a 14,262 crowd. The game was followed by a 1-0 Molineux win over Lazio and then a 3-1 victory away to Fiorentina before Lazio gained revenge with a 2-0 victory in Italy.

More foreign opposition at Molineux (below) in the form of German club Hannover 96, who won 2-1 in August, 1970, in a pre-season friendly. Wolves no 10 Bobby Gould, signed from Arsenal for £55,000 that summer, and keeper Hurst Podlasly do battle in this incident as Bill McGarry's men aimed for top-flight lift-off. Alas, they picked up where they had left off and lost their first three games, conceding ten goals.

The game that started to turn Wolves' fortunes....a 1-0 win at Coventry on August 25, 1970, that was secured by a Hugh Curran goal. Although Wolves lost heavily at Nottingham Forest in their next outing, they then embarked on a run of nine First Division games undefeated. John Holsgrove clears desperately from former Wolves forward Ernie Hunt here, with Derek Parkin and Jim McCalliog as back-up.

Below: Wolves went into the Texaco Cup for the first time in 1970-71 and made uncertain initial progress, following up a 2-1 first-leg win at Dundee in round one by drawing 0-0 with the Scots at Molineux on September 29. Bobby Gould had by now opened his goal account and was close here to adding to it, only for Ronnie Selway to hook clear. The attendance was a respectable 13,042 and there were more when Wolves beat Morton in the next round.

Southampton were unbeaten at home in the League in 1970-71 until Derek Dougan popped up between goalkeeper Eric Martin and Jimmy Gabriel to score this decider in a 2-1 victory in early October. Dave Wagstaffe had levelled the scores a minute before in what was Wolves' fourth successive First Division win. Fortune was on their side at The Dell, though, as Mike Channon's opening goal inside 35 seconds was quickly followed by a miss from the penalty spot by Ron Davies.

Bobby Gould was Molineux man of the moment at the time of this 3-0 victory over Manchester City on October 24, 1970. The striker gets the better of Tony Book (left) and Colin Bell here and scored twice against the holders of the League Cup and European Cup Winners Cup, having hit a hat-trick in a 3-2 win against Manchester United three weeks earlier. Gould's 11th and 12th goals of the season sealed Wolves' sixth successive League success - their best top-flight run since 1957-58.

Left: Bobby Gould savours a goal with Kenny Hibbitt and Mike Bailey while Jim McCalliog indulges in a separate celebration in the background. Happy scenes such as this became common at Molineux in the autumn of 1970, with Wolves' forwards in prolific form and the side making hay near the top of the First Division table.

Below: Early joy for Wolves in their derby clash with Albion at Molineux on November 7, 1970, as Jim Cumbes makes a pig's ear of Dave Wagstaffe's corner and allows it in at his near post. Derek Dougan added the second in a 2-1 victory for a side who had Jim McCalliog at no 7 and Bobby Gould at no 9. Doug Fraser is Albion's no 2. Wolves' six-game League winning run had ended with a 2-0 defeat away to Liverpool the week before.

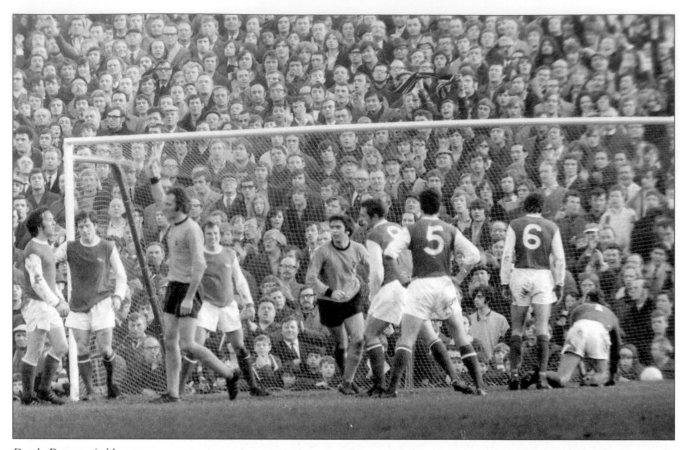

Derek Dougan (with arm raised) and Bobby Gould celebrate the Irishman's headed goal in a losing cause (above) at Highbury on December 12, 1970. Arsenal were 2-0 up when this one went in and the Gunners stayed firm to triumph by the odd goal en route to lifting the League Championship and FA Cup four months later. It was Dougan's first game back following several weeks out injured, the presence of senior strikers such as him restricting John Richards to a meagre seven senior appearances that season. A handful of Wolves fans share the duo's joy in the days when there was no crowd segregation and they were heartened by a spirited performance from their side, who had Phil Parkes (right) to thank for dealing nimbly with this ball into his goalmouth as Bernard Shaw (left) and John McAlle guard his line. The defeat was only Wolves' third in 16 League matches.

League champions Everton had their colours lowered on their Boxing Day visit to Molineux in 1970 as Wolves struck with two second-half Derek Dougan goals without reply, one of them pictured flying in above despite the efforts of keeper Andy Rankin and defender John Hurst. It was a seventh victory in eight Division One home matches for Wolves, who were well in the running for a European place.

Centre: Kenny Hibbitt stretches to put Wolves in front for the second time in their FA Cup third-round tie at home to Second Division Norwich on January 2, 1971. The score was 1-1 at half-time but the second half went all one-way as the favourites cruised home 5-1. At that time, both home and away teams changed colours in the competition in the event of a clash, hence Wolves' appearance in white shirts.

Left: Appeals from both sides as Wolves have a goal disallowed in their 2-1 League victory at Derby on January 9, 1971. The decision went against Derek Dougan, with Kenny Hibbitt as his animated team-mate. The Rams keeper is Colin Boulton and skipper Dave Mackay and Roy McFarland are his grateful defenders. Derby still lost to goals by Bobby Gould and Bernard Shaw (one of only two he scored in 156 Wanderers games) on a day when the players wore black armbands following the death of 66 fans in a disaster at Ibrox Park. Wolves didn't have long to wait to sample the cloying Baseball Ground mud again....

Stirring images from the FA Cup round-four tie in a Baseball Ground mudbath on January 23, 1971. Wolves had won 2-1 at the venue in the League a fortnight earlier and again played well in the sudden-death format. Despite falling behind to a penalty by their former winger Alan Hinton, they rallied to equalise in the second half as John Richards left Derby keeper Colin Boulton open-mouthed in despair (above) by bundling in the equaliser after Derek Dougan had hit the bar. It was the young striker's first goal in the FA Cup but his joy was short-lived. Although Wolves survived this scare (below) as John O'Hare got in between John McAlle and Derek Parkin to threaten Phil Parkes' goal, the same Derby striker popped up to score a last-gasp winner for Brian Clough's side.

This single-goal victory at home to FA Cup holders Chelsea lifted Wolves into third place on February 13, 1971. Kenny Hibbitt was the match-winner and set off here through the snowflakes to celebrate his 55th minute goal. He had also scored at Stamford Bridge earlier that season in his first senior start for the club. Wolves had been third from bottom at the end of August.

Happy scenes from Wolves' thrilling 4-2 victory away to Albion in the centenary meeting of the old Black Country rivals on March 20, 1971. It was a third win in four derbies for the men from Molineux, with the other one drawn, and they were too hot for the Baggies to hold on a mudbath of a surface that tested both teams. Hugh Curran was the hero of the hour as he scored twice en route to a season's haul of 20 goals, this run in behind John Kaye in Albion's well-manned defence bringing him joy with a sharp downward header that bounced past keeper Jim Cumbes. Curran, who was to win five Scottish caps, scored twice in five minutes early in the second half - good enough reason for this extravagant celebration (inset) in front of the away fans in the Smethwick End. Man of the match, though, was winger Dave Wagstaffe, who was outstanding on Wolves' left up against Albion's makeshift right-back John Kaye.

Three goals in the last 16 minutes saw Wolves crush Derry City 4-0 in the semi-final of the short-lived Texaco Cup on March 23, 1971. The competition, for sides from England, Scotland and Northern Ireland, was won by Bill McGarry's side, who took the lead with this goal from Derek Parkin after they had won the first leg 1-0 in Ulster nearly four months earlier. Wolves beat Hearts 3-2 on aggregate in the final, winning 3-1 in the first leg at Tynecastle, having launched their run with two-leg victories over Dundee and Morton.

Having won 2-1 at Everton to record a tremendous double over the League champions, Wolves scented another big scalp at Old Trafford two days later on Easter Monday. But they missed their chances and it was Manchester United who scored the winner just before half-time through Alan Gowling (far right). Phil Parkes, supported by John McAlle and Mike Bailey, punches clear here from George Best.

Two goals in three first-half minutes gave Bill McGarry a winning return to Leeds Road on April 24, 1971. The manager spent ten playing years at Huddersfield, who were nearing the end of the first of their two seasons back in the top flight when they were beaten by strikes from Hugh Curran and Jim McCalliog. Mike O'Grady, on the right as Bernard Shaw clears, and Derek Parkin were also going 'home.'

Having qualified for Europe by finishing fourth in 1970-71 - their highest top-flight placing for ten years - Wolves had an extra spring in their step when they trained at Dunstall Park racecourse in the following July in their build-up to the new season. Manager Bill McGarry shows himself to be capable of keeping up as Jim McCalliog and John McAlle set a hot pace turning into the home straight. Leading the chasing pack are Les Wilson, Derek Parkin and Danny Hegan, the latter signed a year or so earlier from the manager's ex-club Ipswich.

A celebratory note on which to start 1971-72 as Wolves do battle with League Cup holders Tottenham at Molineux on August 14. Jim McCalliog salutes the South Bank masses after Bobby Gould (right) had crashed his shot past Mike England for goal no 1. McCalliog himself added the second from a penalty and Wolves still led 2-0 with 14 minutes left, only for Spurs to rally and salvage a point.

Wolves lost 3-2 to Liverpool in their first trip of 1971-72 before taking a good point away to Leeds four days later. The game was switched to Huddersfield with Elland Road closed as a punishment following serious crowd trouble the previous spring and Jack Charlton went as close as most to breaking the deadlock with this header that sailed away from Phil Parkes, John McAlle and Bernard Shaw but to safety.

Wolves were well into their stride when they took on Everton at Molineux on September 11, 1971, having won three and drawn one of their previous four League games. Derek Dougan had scored only once to date but threatens here as England defender Keith Newton and the grounded Gordon West watch an effort go close. Wolves' goalscorer was Danny Hegan but Harry Catterick's Everton - League champions just over 12 months earlier - escaped with a point from a 1-1 draw.

Derek Dougan, watched by no 9 and fellow scorer Jim McCalliog, times his leap perfectly to head the first of his three goals in Wolves' 4-2 home victory over Nottingham Forest on September 25, 1971. Bill McGarry's side had been struggling to find a cutting edge in the League but suddenly found scoring easier. The keeper is Jim Barron, previously of Wolves and later to return as their assistant manager.

John McAlle (no 6) celebrates opening the scoring in Wolves' first European tie for ten years - the UEFA Cup clash with Academica Coimbra in September, 1971. The competition replaced the Inter Cities Fairs Cup and Bill McGarry's side made the most emphatic of progress as they won 3-0 and 4-1, although Danny Hegan was sent off in an away leg in which Derek Dougan scored his second hat-trick in five days. McAlle scored only three goals in 508 Wolves games and, remarkably, all of them came in September, 1971. He netted home and away against Coimbra and also in a League Cup defeat at Manchester City.

Coventry centre-half Jeff Blockley appeals successfully for offside as Derek Dougan finds himself confronted by keeper Bill Glazier in the 1-1 First Division draw between the Midlands rivals at Molineux on October 30, 1971. Willie Carr, later to move to Molineux, netted for the Sky Blues and Frank Munro for a Wolves side whose League fortunes were still up and down, although they had followed up their 7-1 thrashing of Academica Coimbra by winning 3-1 away to Dutch club Den Haag in the first leg of the UEFA Cup's second round.

# RIP
## Derek Dougan
(1938 to 2007)

Top: Denied by the Locomotiv Leipzig keeper as Wolves go close to turning round their 3-0 UEFA Cup round-two deficit in the autumn of 1973.

Left: Striding out at Molineux and getting the better of one of his old adversaries - Albion's John Kaye.

Top: Sharing a shower with a friend. Dougan and Spurs goalkeeper Pat Jennings; Northern Ireland allies.

Middle: Hero to a gold and black generation.

Bottom: Displaying courage aplenty with a headed winner away to Coventry in October, 1968.

Above: A threat on the ground, in this instance in a game at Crystal Palace.

Left: A menace in the air, as discovered at Molineux by Palace defender John Craven.

Below: Part of the formidable backbone of Wolves' side in the early 1970s.

John McAlle shepherds the ball away from Kevin Hector in Wolves' thrilling 2-1 win over Derby on November 13, 1971. Wolves came from behind with John Richards' brace to remain unbeaten at home in all competitions and inflict only a second defeat of the season on Brian Clough's men, who would look hopefully towards Molineux six months later. Jim McCalliog (left) and Mike Bailey stand by here.

It didn't get much better than when double winners Arsenal were blown away by five goals in 20 second-half minutes on this magical snowy Molineux afternoon on November 20, 1971. Wolves trailed before winning 5-1 and having Barry Davies eulogising on Match of the Day, Derek Dougan squeezing the third past Sammy Nelson and keeper Bob Wilson here from a tight angle for one of his two.

Two images of another high-scoring Wolves victory. Above: John Richards (right) turns away as Jim McCalliog salutes his second minute opener against relegation-threatened Albion at The Hawthorns on November 27, 1971. Alistair Robertson, destined to move to Molineux 15 years later, is the grimacing defender on the right. Below: Robertson is again unable to intervene as Richards bullets a right-foot shot past John Osborne for what proved to be the decider in the visitors' 3-2 triumph - a successful return to the domestic scene after they had travelled to East Germany in midweek and won 1-0 against Carl Zeiss Jena in the third round of the UEFA Cup. This League derby brought Albion the fourth in a run of seven successive defeats under their new manager, Wolverhampton-born Don Howe.

It was a night for anoraks when Wolves swamped East German amateurs and league leaders Carl Zeiss Jena on December 8, 1971. The 3-0 home win completed a 4-0 aggregate success and took the two-goal Derek Dougan past Peter Broadbent as the club's highest scorer in Europe. Wolves, with John McAlle and John Richards challenging here, thus also equalled Leeds' record of six successive Euro wins.

Gordon Banks retrieves the ball from his net after Derek Dougan had beaten him to help set up Wolves' 2-0 League victory over Stoke at Molineux on December 18, 1971. Kenny Hibbitt, with arm outstretched, and no 7 Jim McCalliog are the players ready to add their congratulations on an afternoon when Wolves were also helped by an Andy Bloor own goal as they extended their unbeaten sequence in the League and cups to eight matches - a run that would stretch to 12 before an FA Cup replay defeat at Leicester.

League leaders Manchester United were brought down to earth by a tremendous Wolves performance on January 8, 1972. Derek Dougan outjumps Paul Edwards here to head the visitors into an early lead and John Richards, on his first appearance at Old Trafford, made it two before Jim McCalliog completed a 3-1 victory with a penalty against the club he would later join. David Sadler (left) is powerless to prevent Wolves' first step towards a fourth successive Division One victory after other wins against Stoke, Leicester and Newcastle.

Wolves defend in depth on their way to a 0-0 draw at Coventry on February 19, 1972, although they find luck on their side with this disallowed Ian St John goal. Derek Parkin joins Phil Parkes to patrol the line and Derek Dougan, Frank Munro, John McAlle and no 4 Gerry Taylor are also in attendance to help protect a third clean sheet in four games, the exception being a 5-2 defeat at Manchester City.

# The Great European Adventure

No European tie stands out prouder in Wolverhampton Wanderers' history than this one, when they beat Juventus over two legs in the 1971-72 UEFA Cup quarter-final. They had the legendary John Charles as their interpreter for the first-leg trip to Turin and his skills were needed to smooth out this difference of opinion (above). Bill McGarry's side held the Italian giants 1-1 thanks to a goal by Jim McCalliog and may even have come back to England in the lead had Danny Hegan not narrowly been beaten (left) to this centre.

Wolves enthralled a 40,000-plus crowd by winning 2-1 in an unforgettable return leg against Juventus and going through to the last four of a major European tournament for only the second time. This time the feat followed a lengthy tour of the Continent that had also taken them to Portugal, Holland and East Germany. McCalliog further threatens the Italian defence in this raid (above) from the Molineux leg while (right) a run by Dave Wagstaffe is in full flight. Hegan and Derek Dougan scored to secure the 3-2 aggregate win that took Wolves through.

Two crucial moments from the UEFA Cup semi-final victory over Ferencvaros in April, 1972. Left: Phil Parkes sticks out a leg and diverts this penalty from Istvan Szoke to safety in a first leg in the giant Nep Stadium in which John Richards' first goal in ten games and Frank Munro's close-range header earned McGarry's men a 2-2 draw. It was fraught at Molineux, too, but the home side's pressure, underlined below as Derek Dougan has the visitors under threat, held sway in paving the way for a 2-1 victory and a 4-3 aggregate triumph. Munro was again on target in the return, the other goal going to Steve Daley, who was starting a European tie for the first time. And there was another penalty save by Parkes from Szoke, who had beaten him from the spot with yet another kick in Budapest. Wolves, at the time, were in a run of four successive defeats in the League.

# McGARRY RULE

The big disappointment for Wolves after their refreshing, goal-laden UEFA Cup travels was that the two-leg final was against Spurs, winners over AC Milan in the other semi. The Londoners took an early grip by winning the first leg 2-1 at Molineux in front of 38,362, Martin Chivers' two goals coming either side of one at the other end by Jim McCalliog. Derek Dougan, so prolific in the earlier rounds of the competition, failed to score in the semi-final or final, although he had Mike England on his toes (top) as Alan Mullery chases back in the distance. A fortnight later, 52,891 packed into White Hart Lane, where Mullery opened the scoring with a header (below) that had Spurs celebrating and sensing glory. They did make it across the finishing line and went close again in the second half (left) but only after Dave Wagstaffe levelled on the night with the 27th goal of Wolves' thrilling march through Europe.

Wolves also had a big part to play in the title race in the spring of 1972. Leeds, FA Cup winners two days earlier, came to Molineux needing a point to win the League and seal the double but Wolves famously won 2-1 in front of 53,379 in a game tinged with controversy over allegations of bribery. Above: It's John McAlle summing up Wolves' 100 per cent commitment by blocking Peter Lorimer's shot, watched by the scorer of the first goal, Frank Munro. The result, coupled with Liverpool's failure to win away to Arsenal, meant Derby were champions - much to the despair of Leeds' skipper and goalscorer Billy Bremner (right) as he leaves the pitch.

Bill McGarry signed a new five-year deal before Wolves, having finished ninth in the top flight as well as contested the first all-English European final, kicked off 1972-73. And they were impressive in the goal-laden late-summer weeks, with John Richards (half hidden) red-hot. It was Danny Hegan who drove this goal past Peter Shilton, though, to earn Wolves a 1-1 draw at Leicester on September 23.

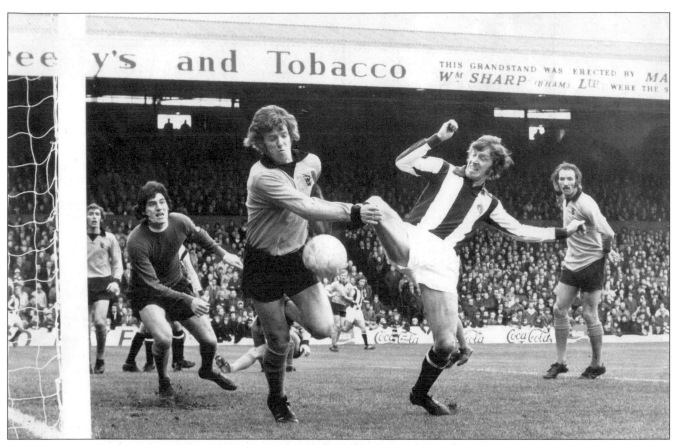

Wolves surprisingly lost their five-match unbeaten League record when they made the short trip to The Hawthorns on October 21, 1972. Albion were struggling and would end the season relegated but took the points on this occasion with a second-half winner from Bobby Gould, the striker who was having a spell at West Brom in between his two Molineux stints. Bernard Shaw has his work cut out here to deny a high-kicking John Wile as John McAlle, Phil Parkes and Derek Dougan look on.

Wolves were again standing above half-way in the First Division table when they handed out this League Cup fourth-round hammering to Third Division Bristol Rovers on October 31, 1972. John Richards slips the ball past Rick Sheppard to open the scoring and the home side added three more through Jim McCalliog (2) and Steve Kindon without reply to avenge the 2-0 win Rovers recorded against them at their former Eastville home in the pre-season Watney Cup. Wolves beat Blackpool in a replay in the next round of the League Cup.

Left: John Richards celebrates his goal in the home League game against Arsenal on November 11, 1972. But the Gunners held firm to win 3-1 and confirm this as a dodgy time for Wolves, who had gone out of the Texaco Cup at Ipswich in midweek after an opening-stage victory over Kilmarnock and who would soon lose at Portman Road in the League - their seventh successive Division One game without a win.

Below: Big moment for Alan Sunderland as he drives home his first-ever League goal past Dave Webb to earn Wolves a 1-0 home victory over Chelsea on December 16, 1972. The Yorkshire lad, who would don nine differently numbered shirts for the club and score a 1979 FA Cup final winner for Arsenal, had been little used in a side whose fortunes began to pick up with good victories at Sheffield United and Everton. Kenny Hibbitt is in support.

Wolves found themselves up against Tottenham once more in December, 1972, this time in the League Cup semi-final. Following earlier KOs of Orient, Sheffield Wednesday, Bristol Rovers and Blackpool, Bill McGarry's side were confronted by their long-time bogey club - one who had caused particular hurt at Molineux in cup football but also in a big League game as far back as 1960 - at a time when they were well placed in the First Division. But they were again unable to squeeze past the talented Londoners, who won 2-1 in the first leg at Molineux despite this successful penalty by Kenny Hibbitt past Pat Jennings. As in the UEFA Cup final only seven months earlier, Wolves fought hard in the second leg at White Hart Lane and emerged with a draw, this own goal by Terry Naylor under pressure from John Richards raising their hopes. The no 9 later finished brilliantly for his 20th goal of the season - one that earned a 2-2 draw on the night and high praise from BBC commentator Barry Davies but not a place in the final against Norwich at Wembley.

Full-back Bernard Shaw, of all people, wheels away as Wolves celebrate one of the goals by which they beat champions-elect Liverpool 2-1 at Molineux on January 27, 1973. John Richards (no 9) and the visitors' no 6 Emlyn Hughes (own goal) made sure of the win that kept the club's winter going on an inconsistent theme, a Molineux loss at the hands of Southampton being followed by a third-round FA Cup win at home to Manchester United.

Wolves had beaten Second Division Bristol City 1-0 with a Mike Bailey strike in the FA Cup fourth round by the time they returned to Molineux to take on Newcastle in the First Division a fortnight later on February 17, 1973. And it proved to be a good afternoon for midfielder Kenny Hibbitt, who opened the scoring with this sweetly-struck right-foot shot midway through the first half and then joined the constabulary on the perimeter track as he milked the applause of the South Bank supporters. Unfortunately, Newcastle breached a home defence by now containing Derek Jefferson to take a point from a 1-1 draw and continue Wolves' up-and-down progress, the Molineux men nevertheless taking maximum points from their next three League matches, away to Birmingham (1-0), at home to Manchester City (5-1) and away to Chelsea (2-0).

Wolves didn't leave much room for error as they progressed in the 1972-73 FA Cup, this fifth-round success at home to Second Division Millwall proving to be their third win out of three by a 1-0 margin in that season's competition. Alan Dorney is the defender not quite able to get across in time (above) as John Richards beats keeper Bryan King from close range to repeat the match-winning contribution he had made against Bristol City in the fourth round three weeks earlier. Below: Steve Daley, in for Dave Wagstaffe for his FA Cup debut, tenaciously battles to keep possession. Wolves were about to hit a rich vein of form in the League by winning four of their next five Division One matches and being drawn at home to Coventry in the FA Cup - a competition in which they had yet to concede a goal.

Molineux's last 50,000 crowd descended on March 17, 1973, to see Wolves take on Coventry in the quarter-final of the FA Cup. And the majority were on their feet when John Richards left Bobby Parker in his wake as he ran through (top) to fire left-footed past the advancing Bill Glazier in the first half. It was the third successive round in which the striker had broken the ice and he would finish the season with an outstanding tally of 36 goals - comfortably the best of his 13-year first-team career at the club. Kenny Hibbitt put the tie to bed with a second-half penalty (middle picture) and Wolves were through to their third major semi-final in two seasons and their first in the FA Cup since 1960. Left: Phil Parkes, no mean performer as a bowler in local club cricket, prepares to throw out as Colin Stein, policed by John McAlle, faces up to him.

Alas, it was semi-final heartbreak once more for Wolves when they travelled to Maine Road, Manchester, to face Cup holders Leeds on April 7. Well though they played - even hitting the inside of the post through a left-foot shot from John Richards when it was still 0-0 well into the second half - they were beaten by a Billy Bremner goal in the latter stages. Richards is on the move (above) as Derek Dougan aims a header at the target while Phil Parkes punches clear (below) under pressure from Mick Jones as Frank Munro, Derek Parkin, Gerry Taylor and Kenny Hibbitt form a gold barrier. Munro played after passing a late fitness test and, with skipper Mike Bailey able only to go on from the substitutes' bench (for Hibbitt) after being another pre-match injury worry, Wolves were left thinking what might have been - especially as Second Division Sunderland reached Wembley and beat Leeds 1-0.

Alan Sunderland exemplified the eventful run-in Wolves had following their FA Cup adventure, scoring four times in the last fortnight of the 1972-73 season as the club finished fifth in the table to once more qualify for the UEFA Cup. Two of those goals came in this 3-0 home victory over Norwich on a muddy Easter Monday, with the forward - by now sporting longer hair - celebrating the opener here. John Richards was also on target.

Left: Plaudits came thick and fast for John Richards at the end of 1973 - and no wonder! He finished the season as the country's top scorer with 36 goals - a haul that prompted England to select him against Northern Ireland at Goodison Park for his only senior cap. Here, popular chairman John Ireland presents him with the Midlands Footballer of the Year Trophy, put up by the Evening Mail, as JR reflects on a year in which the club lost two semi-finals.

Wolves were back in European combat in October, 1973, and soon winning ties home and away again! The first-round draw took them to Belenenses, where they won 2-0 in front of a crowd of only 8,925 despite one of two sendings-off John Richards suffered in his career. The striker scored, along with Derek Dougan, in Portugal and his subsequent suspension let in reserve forward Peter Eastoe to net here in the 2-1 victory in the return at Molineux, where Jim McCalliog was also on target.

East Germany was Wolves' next destination and they were struggling after losing the away leg against Locomotiv Leipzig 3-0 on October 24, 1973. The side built up a good head of steam at Molineux a fortnight later and swept into a 4-1 lead but couldn't find the decisive fifth goal that would have prevented them slipping agonisingly out on the away goals rule. Derek Dougan, on the score-sheet with Frank Munro, Kenny Hibbitt and Steve Kindon, is the frustrated man here as the keeper deals with a cross that Munro also has an eye on.

Left: Mike Bailey and Derek Parkin are caught out by Brian Alderson's flicked header as Wolves defend in the League game at Coventry on December 8, 1973. Frank Munro, marking David Cross at the far post, is quick to react but couldn't prevent Wolves slipping to a 1-0 defeat after they had won 3-1 at Tottenham and drawn 2-2 at Arsenal in their previous two League games. Wolves won 3-2 at Stoke in their next outing.

Molineux's younger look is reflected in this photo (below) from Wolves' 2-1 home League win against Southampton on January 1, 1974, as Alan Sunderland watches Barry Powell, another product of the club's nursery system, go close with a shot. It was the older guard who delivered the goal-scoring goods, though, with Dave Wagstaffe and John Richards on target in a win that extended the side's unbeaten run to six games. Waggy's goal was his first in the League for more than two years while there were decidedly mixed fortunes for his two young team-mates. Powell was stretchered off with knee damage and Sunderland missed a penalty on a day when Mike Channon saw a spot-kick superbly saved by Phil Parkes.

His senior England claims repeatedly overlooked, John Richards had to settle for international crumbs such as this. The unattractive setting is wintry Ashton Gate, Bristol, where JR couldn't quite break the deadlock with this shot in the under-23 clash with Wales in early 1974. Geoff Palmer, Birmingham's Trevor Francis and the Latchford brothers, Peter (WBA) and Bob (Blues), were also in England's side.

At last! After all the near misses, Wolves made it to a major domestic final when they reached Wembley with Manchester City in the 1973-74 League Cup. Victories over Halifax, Tranmere and Exeter in the early rounds were followed by the higher-profile conquest of Liverpool as John Richards scored the only goal, then Wolves leaned on the same marksman for the decider in this semi-final second leg at home to Norwich after the teams had drawn 1-1 at Carrow Road. Celebrating afterwards are (from left) John Richards, Frank Munro, John McAlle, Mike Bailey, Geoff Palmer, Barry Powell, Alan Sunderland and Kenny Hibbitt.

# League Cup Winners

Departing for pre-Wembley HQ are (from left) Bailey, Hibbitt, Munro, McAlle, Daley, Richards, Wagstaffe, Pierce, Parkin, Dougan and (crouching) Sunderland and McCalliog. Wolves had just drawn at Old Trafford, where Pierce saved rival keeper Alex Stepney's penalty.

The friendly four-ball that almost cost Dave Wagstaffe (left) a Wembley place against his old club. Bill McGarry was apparently so angry when he and no 2 Sammy Chung lost to Waggy and Mike Bailey at Worthing, Sussex, that he ordered the players in for afternoon training on their day-off. In practice, Wagstaffe pulled a thigh muscle and was barely fit for the final after hiding the injury from the management.

Wolves' expectant players line up in one of the Wembley goalmouths during their eve-of-final look round the stadium in March, 1974. From left, in some decidedly 1970s gear, are Gary Pierce, John McAlle, Phil Parkes, Steve Daley, Derek Dougan, Frank Munro, Alan Sunderland, Barry Powell, Mike Bailey, John Richards, Geoff Palmer, Derek Parkin, Jim McCalliog, Dave Wagstaffe and Kenny Hibbitt.

City no 8 Colin Bell falls into the arms of Denis Law after driving in the equaliser near the hour mark, much to the despair of John McAlle, Frank Munro, Mike Bailey and the grounded Gary Pierce. Wolves had gone ahead through a sliced volley from Kenny Hibbitt shortly before the half-time break and, with their stand-in goalkeeper absolutely inspired on the day of his 23rd birthday, had one more trick up their sleeve in the form of John Richards' late winner (celebrated by the scorer and Derek Dougan in the smaller picture above).

Right: The injury that inadvertently helped to confirm Wolves as League Cup winners. Dave Wagstaffe is attended by physiotherapist Toby Andersen as the thigh muscle problem he had been nursing for several days takes its toll at Wembley. The popular left-winger, who played 404 games for the club, had to go off to be replaced by Barry Powell - a switch that meant the also-struggling John Richards stayed on and was around to sweep in the 85th minute winner.

Below: I knew you wouldn't let me down! Bill McGarry, having made one of Wembley's more memorable post-match runs, shakes the hands of Gary Pierce before giving his keeper the full hug at the end of Wolves' thrilling 2-1 victory over Manchester City. The Bury-born reserve had come into the side a month or so earlier because of an injury to the unlucky Phil Parkes, who had left Molineux by the time Wolves next reached Wembley - in the 1980 League Cup final. Parkes' comeback came four weeks later, ironically in a 1-1 draw at Manchester City in the First Division.

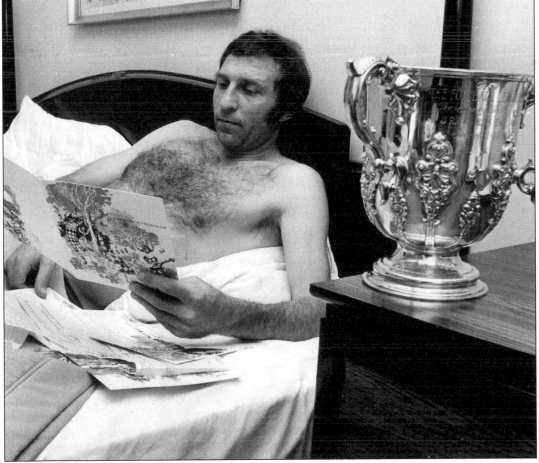

Above: Words are hardly needed......players who had performed for years in the shadow of their 1950s and early 1960s predecessors have some silverware to show at last for several seasons of challenging for major honours. Skipper Mike Bailey and the scorer of the winning goal John Richards have a strong hold on the cup while Gary Pierce (front) looks a little bemused after his man-of-the-match role.

Left: When you take the League Cup to bed with you, that's real pride! Wolves skipper Mike Bailey wakes up with the cherished silverware and a host of congratulatory messages following the famous 2-1 Wembley victory over Manchester City. In an interview for the Official History of Wolves dvd, Bailey said the moment he received the cup was 'shivery.'

A heroes' welcome from the thousands lining the streets near the Town Hall as skipper Mike Bailey disembarks. It was a repeat of the scenes Wolverhampton had become used to in the glory years and which would be mirrored when subsequent sides won at Wembley or the Millennium Stadium. Below: Bailey and Bill McGarry delight the masses by raising the League Cup. McGarry, frustrated by several near misses, later revealed he would have quit had Wolves lost to Manchester City, believing that they were fated not to win a top honour.

Left: John Richards sees to it that John McAlle doesn't let his sartorial standards slip as Wolves' players turn out at the civic banquet in their honour on March 6, 1974. Also pictured are Kenny Hibbitt and Derek Parkin. Richards didn't play again that season because of a knee injury - an absence that allowed Peter Withe to embark on a brief Molineux first-team career that started with a goal in the 3-1 home win over Ipswich.

Below: Still high-spirited…..skipper Mike Bailey measures Bill McGarry for size as a local tailor honours the 1974 League Cup winners by kitting them out with quality suits. Also pictured (from left) are Derek Parkin, Alan Sunderland, Steve Daley, John McAlle (in the background), Barry Powell, Derek Jefferson, Frank Munro, David Wagstaffe and Sammy Chung.

# Ups And Downs

David Cross saves Frank Munro the bother of intervening as he heads an own goal in Wolves' 1-1 home draw with Coventry on April 20, 1974. Although Bill McGarry's side were to lose at Derby in their final game, there was no slacking off in the run-in as they beat Derby (4-0), Arsenal (3-1) and Leicester (1-0) at home in a run of seven games unbeaten that helped them to a final placing of 12th.

European football came once more to Molineux in 1974-75, courtesy of the League Cup win, and the draw sent Wolves to Portugal for the third time in four seasons. Porto were their opponents and formidable ones at that, following up a 4-1 home victory by restricting Wolves to a 3-1 win in the return despite a brilliant performance marked by a Derek Dougan goal. Mike Bailey and Steve Daley were also on target. Wolves' hold on the League Cup had already been ended by a surprise home defeat against Second Division Fulham.

The 1974-75 season was forgettable for Wolves on the cup front, with first-stage elimination in the League and UEFA Cups followed by a third-round exit at home to Ipswich in the FA Cup. The side stayed in mid-table, though, and this 1-0 home win (top) over Arsenal ended a run of four league losses, this Kenny Hibbitt penalty the decider.

Middle: Following a 7-1 humiliation of Chelsea in March on Willie Carr's debut, Kenny Hibbitt was again the hero of the 5-2 victory at home to relegation-bound Luton. Hibbitt netted three times and Peter Withe and Carr once.

Left: Wolves started 1975-76 poorly and drew three and lost three of their first six League matches. The tide started to turn in the next home game against Birmingham on September 13, though. Wolves won 2-0 with a brace by Willie Carr, who is hugged here by Alan Sunderland. In the same month, the side beat Swindon in the League Cup.

It took another clash with Birmingham to lift Wolves' morale - they again ran out 2-0 winners, this time at St Andrew's, in a League Cup tie (above) on October 7, 1975. John McAlle makes a brilliant tackle here to halt Trevor Francis and two goals at the other end by Kenny Hibbitt saw Wolves through to a trip to Mansfield that brought a shock KO. Below: With The Doog gone after 123 goals in 323 games, Hibbitt took his tally to six with a brace in a 5-1 win over fellow strugglers Sheffield United and leapt into the arms of Steve Daley to celebrate (right).

# UPS AND DOWNS

Bobby Gould, who had been re-signed by Wolves towards the end of 1975, squeezes home an angled shot for the equaliser that prised a point from a 1-1 draw against Leeds at home in January, 1976. Paul Madeley is the defender and Scot David Harvey - previously a target for Wolves - is the beaten goalkeeper. There were signs of improvement at the time from Wolves after they thrashed Arsenal 3-0 in the FA Cup and won at Birmingham in the League.

Another moment of fleeting hope for Wolves.....John Richards outwits Graham Oates on his way to scoring a hat-trick in a 5-0 slaughter of Newcastle on April 10, 1976. Kenny Hibbitt and Willie Carr also found the net for Bill McGarry's men, who had gamely reached the quarter-final of the FA Cup before losing in a Molineux replay to Manchester United. In the final match under the manager, Wolves were to famously lose 3-1 in front of a 48,918 crowd at home to a Liverpool side who thus clinched the title. While the Merseysiders celebrated, Wolves were coming to terms with the reality of relegation after nine top-flight years. Frank Munro is also pictured.

A spring in which Wolves also lost to Albion in the FA Youth Cup final saw Bill McGarry's long-time assistant Sammy Chung appointed in his place. Chung (left), a more placid individual and recognised as a good coach, found himself working with an unchanged squad for the 1976-77 Division Two season. Bobby Gould extended a welcoming hand on the first day of pre-season training, when (from left) John Farley, Willie Carr, Derek Parkin and Geoff Palmer were also happy to join in the banter.

The League Cup proved unrewarding for Wolves after their 1974 Wembley glory, Third Division side Sheffield Wednesday removing them at the first hurdle in August, 1976, after similar conquests by Fulham and Mansfield in the previous two seasons. Big Steve Kindon, signed from Burnley to help fill the gap caused by Derek Dougan's retirement, was close with this header on an evening when Derek Parkin's goal proved only light relief in a 2-1 KO. In the league, Wolves began well by going six matches without defeat.

Gary Pierce dives at the feet of Les Bradd in the League game at Notts County on November 13, 1976. Geoff Palmer is the defender lending cover but Wolves needed a last-minute goal by substitute Bobby Gould - his seventh of the season - to rescue a point. At home to Blackburn a week later, John Richards ended a six-month absence following knee surgery by playing his first Second Division game.

Wolves were well into their promotion-chasing stride when they beat Plymouth 4-0 at an icy Molineux on December 4, 1976. Alan Sunderland was denied here by Argyle keeper Neil Ramsbottom but scored along with the lurking John Richards (2) while Kenny Hibbitt also made it on to the score-sheet. The goals were certainly flying in, Wolves having won 4-2 at Orient the previous week, when Richards hit a hat-trick. Sunderland had scored three at home to Carlisle in October.

Above: Wolves clearly relished facing Sheffield United in the mid-1970s and could afford this Kenny Hibbitt miss as they beat them for the third time in four meetings, with the other drawn, in February, 1977. John Richards and Alan Sunderland each netted in a 2-1 victory at Molineux and ended with 20 and 16 goals respectively in a campaign in which Hibbitt (18), Steve Daley (14) and Bobby Gould (10) also reached double figures. The defeated Blades keeper is Jim Brown.

Above: Martin Patching bears down on Bristol Rovers' goal on one of the few occasions Wolves didn't score in their 5-1 victory at Eastville on December 27, 1976! Steve Daley, Ken Hibbitt, Steve Kindon and Alan Sunderland (2) all found a way through as Sammy Chung's men set up one of no fewer than six doubles they managed that season. This success took the club's goal tally to 17 in only five matches from the end of November. Rovers lost 1-0 at Molineux in the March.

Left: Promotion was very much on the agenda when Fulham were well and truly put to the sword at Molineux on February 19, 1977. Even with Bobby Moore, here sidestepping keeper Gerry Peyton, in a line-up that also included George Best and Rodney Marsh, the Londoners crashed to a 5-1 defeat as Steve Daley and Kenny Hibbitt both bagged braces and John Richards also netted. Martin Patching is the forward getting down to action in the Wolverhampton mud.

Above: Steve Daley marks his 100th League game for Wolves by scoring with a long-range header from Willie Carr's corner in the nervous 2-1 win over Blackpool on March 1, 1977 - the side's sixth successive home victory and the 16th leg of an unbeaten run that was to end away to Luton the following week. Following an equaliser by their former striker Bob Hatton, Wolves still needed Kenny Hibbitt's goal four minutes from the end to beat the Seasiders and so leapfrog Bolton into second place, level on points with leaders Chelsea - but, crucially, with two games in hand. Wearing no 9, as he did for much of the season, is the free-scoring Alan Sunderland.

Left: John Richards, who spent much of the 1976-77 season in the no 8 shirt, is beaten by a hefty punch in Wolves' mid-March win over Hereford - their seventh successive home League success. Youngster Kenny Todd and Kenny Hibbitt (also pictured) netted in a 2-1 victory that secured the double over a club who were not that long out of non-league football, Sammy Chung's side having spectacularly won 6-1 at Edgar Street in early October - a result they promptly followed up by losing 6-2 at home to Southampton!

Below: John Richards beats the outstretched leg of visiting defender Stuart Croft to score one of the goals by which Wolves defeated Hull 2-1 on March 26, 1977, and so remained narrow leaders of the Second Division. Richards' 16th goal of an injury-hit campaign opened the scoring just past the hour in a game shown on that night's Match of the Day and was followed by what proved to be the winner from Kenny Hibbitt. Disappointingly, the gate fell below 20,000 for the first time since Christmas.

Wolves were in throwaway mood in this Easter Monday clash, 1977, taking control with goals by Steve Daley and John Richards before Notts County struck either side of half-time to snatch a draw. Daley's goal, driven past Eric McManus here, was one of 14 he managed from midfield that season. The result left Wolves top on goal difference with two home games in hand on closest pursuers Chelsea.

Wolves met relegation-threatened Cardiff twice in 17 days in April, 1977, and were upset not to take full points. In the clash at Ninian Park (above), where Steve Kindon takes evasive action, they had a late shock when two up through Steve Daley and substitute Kenny Hibbitt and then pegged back, the equaliser coming with almost the last kick of the game. Right: John Richards challenges during the Molineux return in which Geoff Palmer hit his first goal of the season and Martin Patching, Alan Sunderland and Kenny Hibbitt also scored in a 4-1 win that meant Sammy Chung's side would have to lose their four remaining games to miss out on promotion.

Wolves were saved by a late goalline clearance in their promotion-sealing 0-0 draw at Plymouth on April 30, 1977. Keeper Gary Pierce, who had played almost 50 senior games in a row but who would be shut out by Phil Parkes and Paul Bradshaw for all of 1977-78, looks round anxiously as the ball bounces in his six-yard area, with no 10 Martin Patching and Frank Munro looking on. Wolves were up with three games to spare but the Second Division Championship was still up for grabs.

Big smiles from Wolves' squad back at Molineux as they reflect on the winning of promotion two days earlier. Pictured by the team coach before training are (from left) Steve Daley, Derek Parkin, Bobby Gould, Willie Carr, Kenny Hibbitt, Geoff Palmer, John Richards, Martin Patching and the crouching Frank Munro. A side containing League debutant Colin Brazier visited Southampton the following night for part two of a south coast double date and lost 1-0. Wolves returned to The Dell for a friendly three months later, this time drawing 0-0.

Left: The title clincher! John Richards celebrates with a packed North Bank after hitting the 77th minute goal that earned Wolves a 1-1 draw with Chelsea and made them Division Two champions. As they returned in style to the top flight after one year away, Chelsea graduated, too, as runners-up. Tommy Langley, later to move to Molineux, opened the scoring on a day that was marked by George Berry's senior debut.

Middle: Frank Munro, in the last of his 371 Wanderers games, closes down Neil Whatmore in a hurry during the 1-0 win at Bolton on the final day of 1976-77. Martin Patching, Derek Parkin, Geoff Palmer and Gary Pierce also bar the way to goal following Kenny Hibbitt's 20th minute winner. Bolton couldn't get the points they needed to go up instead of Brian Clough's Nottingham Forest and missed out on a promotion place on the last afternoon for the second season running.

Bottom: Gary Pierce in the firing line again at Burnden as he dives bravely at the feet of Neil Whatmore to help protect Wolves' narrow lead. The keeper, although injured and replaced in goal by Bobby Gould for the last couple of minutes, was an ever-present that season in taking his tally of successive appearances past 50 but wouldn't play again until October, 1978, because of the form of Phil Parkes and in particular Paul Bradshaw.

# New Division, New Hope

Both teams had a Phil Parkes in their goal in Wolves' first home game back in the top flight in August, 1977 - and Molineux's keeper department also included Gary Pierce and a Chris Pearce! Wanderers opened with a 3-2 win at Bristol City before John Richards, seen here troubling the QPR quintet of Parkes, Dave Webb, Dave Needham and Ian Gillard as Steve Kindon looks on, scored the only goal of the Tuesday-night follow-up fixture. Wolves would complete the League double by winning 3-1 at Loftus Road on New Year's Eve.

John Richards scored his 100th League goal with a header against West Ham on October 15, 1977, when Wolves were having some teething troubles in the big league. Although the striker had rattled in a hat-trick at home to Leicester just before and would net a brace at Manchester City shortly after, the side were held to a 2-2 draw here and were having mixed fortunes. The home no 10 is Norman Bell.

St Andrew's for once did not prove a happy hunting ground for Wolves on Bonfire Night afternoon in 1977 when they were beaten 2-1 by Birmingham, Trevor Francis ushering them towards defeat with this header over Paul Bradshaw. Wolves' goal came from Martin Patching - pictured to the left of the in-rushing Gary Emmanuel - and the side had won only two out of 12 League games since their two opening wins.

Below: Recognise the defender failing to stop Steve Daley driving in one of Wolves' goals at a wintry Molineux on January 21, 1978? It's none other than Dave Jones, later to manage Wolves but back then an Everton player. Up in support with the scorer is striker Norman Bell.

Bottom: No 10 Bell stands back as Kenny Hibbitt scores one of the two goals he plundered in that game against Everton. Sammy Chung's team were keeping their heads above water despite another shock early League Cup exit (at home to Luton) and early FA Cup elimination at Arsenal.

Safe handling by Paul Bradshaw as the former Blackburn keeper demonstrates the form that prompted Phil Parkes' departure from Molineux after 382 senior games. This awkward catch came in Wolves' 3-1 defeat at Derby on April 8, 1978, and denied Don Masson and Terry Curran as John McAlle and Derek Parkin cover. Martin Patching scored for a visiting side who were still in relegation danger.

Best seat in the house! John Richards tucks in his first League goal since Boxing Day in Wolves' 3-1 win over Aston Villa in their last home game of 1977-78. This effort and others by Mel Eves and Billy Rafferty killed off any lingering relegation fears for a side who then won at Ipswich to finish 15th. Jimmy Rimmer is Villa's keeper and Ken McNaught (centre) and Allan Evans the defenders.

Aston Villa are again the opponents, this time in the Second City on the first day of the 1978-79 campaign, as Derek Parkin launches himself into the fray to head behind for a corner under pressure from rival no 4 Allan Evans. John McAlle, Paul Bradshaw and Bob Hazell are the attentive team-mates on an afternoon when Wolves gave a debut to Peter Daniel, the midfielder who had been signed by Sammy Chung from Hull that summer. Villa avenged their May defeat at Molineux by winning 1-0.

Alarmingly, Wolves lost 11 of their first 14 League games of 1978-79 and made yet another first-stage League Cup exit when beaten by the only goal at Fourth Division Reading. The slide spelled the end of Sammy Chung's tenure and John Barnwell had been recruited from Peterborough by the time of this 2-1 Boxing Day home victory over near-neighbours Birmingham. Norman Bell and Mel Eves lead the charge here, although the goals came from midfielders Peter Daniel and Kenny Hibbitt.

Wolves had to work hard to dig themselves out of relegation trouble in the winter of 1978-79, almost literally so in this snow-bound 1-0 victory at home to high-riding Everton on February 3. Geoff Palmer, who would play a total of 496 first-team matches in his two spells at Molineux, is watched by Peter Daniel and no 6 George Berry as he slides in to dispossess the former Burnley midfielder Martin Dobson on a day when Steve Daley's goal gave Wolves their third win in five games. The major uplift in form considerably raised morale at the club and fanned the flames of hope in the survival battle. This was only the third League game Wolves played in an Arctic start to 1979.

Along with their League climb, Wolves were progressing well in the FA Cup and knocked out Brighton, Newcastle and Crystal Palace before being pitched into a romantic quarter-final against Graham Turner's Shrewsbury in March, 1979. The sides drew 1-1 in front of 40,946 at Molineux, Billy Rafferty scoring for Wolves, before this goal by Willie Carr and others by Peter Daniel and Rafferty again sealed a 3-1 replay win at Gay Meadow. Turner is pictured second left as George Berry begins the celebrations.

Wolves' first FA Cup semi-final outing for six years had the cameramen flocking to Molineux in the countdown to the March 31 Villa Park showdown against Arsenal, who had last won the competition since 1971. Pictured are Willie Carr, Peter Daniel, Derek Parkin, Billy Rafferty, John Richards, John McAlle, George Berry, Paul Bradshaw, Steve Daley, Martin Patching, Geoff Palmer and Kenny Hibbitt.

What might have been a golden day for Wolves turned into abject misery as they performed unrecognisably from the way they became used to playing under John Barnwell. John Richards is denied here by the juggling of the unflappable Pat Jennings in a first-half attack.

It was still 0-0 well into the second half at Villa Park but it was perhaps inevitable that Wolves' 2-0 defeat to Arsenal should be sealed by Alan Sunderland, the forward who left them for Highbury for £240,000 some 18 months earlier. Right: Sunderland is the man chasing back to try to cut out this Willie Carr cross. Middle: John Barnwell had to go on the pitch at the end to console the dejected Willie Carr, Billy Rafferty, Peter Daniel and John Richards. It really was that sort of day. In the other semi, Manchester United - managed by Tommy Docherty - beat Liverpool but then lost 3-2 to Arsenal at Wembley, with Sunderland of all people scoring a dramatic late winner!

Below: An ever-hungry John Richards is denied close in by Ray Clemence as Wolves' game with Liverpool on April 10, 1979, runs true to form. Although John Barnwell's team were to win their survival battle and finish 18th in the table, they weren't able to do anything to check the Merseysiders' march towards a fourth League crown in the 1970s. The visitors won 1-0 and finished eight points clear of Nottingham Forest. Also seen here are Billy Rafferty and Liverpool defenders Alan Hansen and a partially-hidden Phil Thompson.

Another valuable point towards top-flight safety as Wolves emerge from their April 21 League game at Albion with a useful 1-1 draw. The spring of 1979 was an exciting time in the Black Country with John Barnwell in charge at Molineux and Ron Atkinson presiding at The Hawthorns, where John Richards - back at the ground where he made his Wanderers debut nine years earlier - had full consolation for being beaten to the ball here by Tony Godden by heading his side's goal. Keeping a close eye on proceedings is Alistair Robertson.

John Richards glances in Steve Daley's left-wing cross to give Wolves a 1-0 home victory over Nottingham Forest on April 30, 1979 - six days after they had thrashed Derby 4-0 and a month before Brian Clough's men won the European Cup for the first time. It was Forest's only defeat in any competition after Boxing Day that season. This header was hailed by some as Richards' 100th First Division goal but that milestone, in fact, came a week later in a 3-2 defeat against Manchester United at Old Trafford. At this time, manager John Barnwell was starting his recovery from potentially life-saving injuries suffered in a serious car crash.

# A Splash Of Gray

Wouldn't you know it! Seven weeks on from his British transfer record move across the Midlands, Wolves' new capture Andy Gray nets against his old club Villa in a 1-1 League draw at Molineux in October, 1979. It was the Scot's second home goal for the club but he had also scored three times away in a period of great hope for the side. No 7 is Kenny Hibbitt while Dennis Mortimer, Allan Evans and keeper Jimmy Rimmer are three of the despairing opponents. It was the 100th competitive clash between Wolves and Villa - and memorable for the wrong reason for John Richards. He was sent off with his marker Brendan Ormsby. This was also the weekend during which Dave Wagstaffe, a Blackburn player for several years after leaving Molineux, was forced to retire on medical advice.

Andy Gray, one of the catalysts for Wolves' excellent 1979-80 season after his sensational switch of clubs in the September, turns away while opening the scoring in the League Cup quarter-final replay with Grimsby at Molineux on December 11. The Third Division club, having forced a 0-0 draw in the first meeting at blustery Blundell Park, bounced back, though, to force a third match, this time on neutral territory, after Wolves had despatched Burnley, Palace and QPR in the earlier rounds.

There were no mistakes by Wolves at the third time of asking, their 2-0 victory over Grimsby at Derby being secured by goals from John Richards and Kenny Hibbitt (penalty), who is seen in support of Andy Gray in attack (above). Scottish international Gray had already scored nine times for his new club, including efforts in thrilling victories at Everton, Arsenal and Manchester City. Below: Hibbitt keeps his nerve to score from the spot as Gray is poised in case of any crumbs. Hibbitt's appearance haul for the club of 574 leaves him second only to Derek Parkin in the all-time list and he scored 114 goals - a tally bettered by only nine others.

Wolves certainly had the luck of the draw in the 1979-80 League Cup, with Third Division Swindon (the 1969 winners) their semi-final opponents while Nottingham Forest faced Bristol City. Even so, John Barnwell's side made heavy weather of it, losing 2-1 at the County Ground in the first leg despite a Peter Daniel equaliser and this break that had John Richards homing in towards Jimmy Allen's goal.

Swindon wouldn't go quietly in the second leg either and Wolves could find no way through in a first half in which John Richards and Andy Gray bore down towards the target. Class eventually told, though, and Mel Eves broke the ice before Richards - the club's all-time leading marksman in the competition - netted twice after the Wiltshire side had equalised. It finished 3-1 on the night and 4-3 overall.

John Richards was fit again and buzzing in 1979-80 and powered this goal low past Ray Clemence from a Peter Daniel through ball as a Liverpool side on the way to retaining their Championship crown were defeated 1-0 at Molineux on February 26. Wolves had won by the same score away to Manchester United in the same month, the only down-side being their 3-0 eclipse in the FA Cup at Molineux by Graham Taylor's Watford.

## Wolves - Wembley Winners Again

Nottingham Forest, League champions in 1978, European Cup winners in 1979 and destined to take the Continent's biggest prize again in 1980, were hot favourites to beat Wolves at Wembley on March 15 and retain the League Cup they had lifted in both 1978 and 1979. But John Barnwell, working his way back to health following a serious car crash, and his assistant Richie Barker set their side up in such a way as to stifle Brian Cough's men and then try to catch them on the break. The tactics worked perfectly, Wolves surviving in relative comfort and then winning the game when a mix-up between David Needham and his keeper Peter Shilton left Andy Gray with the simplest of tap-ins mid-way through the second half. Gray had his sights on goal earlier when Shilton gathered (above) while Mel Eves worried Needham, Ian Bowyer and Kenny Burns (below) when getting between them in another attack.

Wolves were often under the cosh at Wembley but resisted manfully, with keeper Paul Bradshaw including this safe catch from off Kenny Burns' head in an highly impressive personal contribution.

Left: The big moment - duly hailed by Andy Gray. From the left, John Richards, Mel Eves and Peter Daniel are off in excited pursuit of Wolves' match-winner, who gives the supporters a close-up of the celebrations.

Below: With his name up in bright lights in his eye-line, Andy Gray chases back and confronts Martin O'Neill as Wolves battle to protect their valuable lead. Kenny Hibbitt is also on hand.

Let the party begin! Goal-maker Peter Daniel (left) and Black Country boy Mel Eves are wide-mouthed in awe at the sight of the celebrating Wolves masses as the League Cup is shown off round one end of Wembley (left) while the distant terrace empties of thousands of Forest fans. Keeper Paul Bradshaw looks altogether more laid-back about it all and Derek Parkin mulls over whether this winners' experience is better than the first one in 1974. Eves had scored a League decider at Old Trafford a few weeks earlier and came up with a couple of important goals in the cup run - one at Crystal Palace in round three and the other in the second leg of the semi-final against Swindon. Below: It's the rear view of no 4 Daniel - a virtual ever-present in his first two years at the club - and no 11 Eves as they and their team-mates get in even closer contact with the delirious supporters.

We said we wouldn't come back without the trophy! Wolves' players revel in the obligatory open-top bus tour as they return to Wolverhampton. For one player, the happy occasion was especially significant. As a Liverpool stalwart, Emlyn Hughes had won nearly everything the game could throw at him but had repeatedly missed out on League Cup glory until moving from Anfield to Molineux in the summer of 1979.

He is seen waving from the front left as the bus inches its way through Queen Square (left picture) and is crouching in the left of the foreground (below) as the players allow 12-year-old spina bifida victim Vincent Roper to take centre stage with the silverware. Also pictured are (from left) Norman Bell, substitute Colin Brazier, keeper Paul Bradshaw, Derek Parkin, John Richards, George Berry, Mel Eves, Willie Carr, Andy Gray, Kenny Hibbitt and Geoff Palmer.

Exactly a week on from Wembley, Andy Gray strikes again as Wolves beat Stoke 3-0 in front of a 27,968 crowd to maintain their lofty League placing. Mel Eves and John Richards also netted as if to underline the club's attacking options, Richards then picking up a brace in a 3-1 victory at Coventry as a fourth successive Midlands scalp was collected, Aston Villa having been conquered 3-1 on their own pitch only five days before John Barnwell's men set foot at the twin towers.

A helping hand for Wolves in their home game against Manchester City on April 12, 1980, as their former midfielder Steve Daley heads into his own net under pressure from no 10 Wayne Clarke. City overcame the setback to win 2-1 but Wolves ended the season strongly by losing only once more, against Arsenal, as John Richards finished with a haul of 18 - his best since bagging 25 in the 1975-76 relegation year. It was Daley's sale to City for what briefly stood as a British record fee that had enabled Wolves to buy Andy Gray.

Wolves' final position of sixth in 1979-80 left them four places above Albion, whom they met at The Hawthorns only a week into the new season. John Barnwell's team had started by losing at Brighton, as they often did, and winning at home to Manchester United and were content enough with a 1-1 draw in the derby, secured by an Andy Gray goal. Emlyn Hughes is the man under pressure here as John Deehan tries to get behind him and George Berry in a first-half Albion attack.

Wolves tended to either win the League Cup in the mid-1970s and early 1980s or crash at the first hurdle! In September, 1980, it was the latter as they suffered a shock 4-1 defeat over two legs against Second Division Cambridge, who survived this powerful shot by Wayne Clarke, watched by Andy Gray, to add a 1-0 Molineux triumph to the 3-1 victory they had pulled off at the Abbey Stadium a week earlier.

League Cup glory put Wolves back in Europe and they travelled to Holland when they were paired with PSV Eindhoven in the first round of the 1980-81 UEFA Cup. Things were looking good when Andy Gray, drawing on his Continental experience with Aston Villa, had Mel Eves celebrating with a headed equaliser early in the second half (above) of a game that was watched by almost 30,000. The scoreboard on the stand roof was still showing 1-1 when George Berry launched himself at a centre to get in this promising header (below) that further threatened the Dutchmen's goal. But he was out of luck and Wolves were left with an uphill second-leg task when they conceded twice more, once from a penalty, to lose 3-1 on the night. They had rallied superbly to almost overturn even bigger deficits against Porto and Locomotiv Leipzig in the mid-1970s and now needed a similar effort against the odds.

League Cup winners met League champions-elect at Villa Park on September 20, 1980, with the home side running out 2-1 winners. Wolves keeper Paul Bradshaw gets a buffeting here from former Molineux striker Peter Withe as Willie Carr and Emlyn Hughes look on. Mel Eves scored for Wolves but couldn't prevent this fourth successive defeat for his side, including their midweek trip to Holland.

Wolves gave it their all in the return against Eindhoven on October 1, 1980. Having lost all six of their matches in September, they hit some much-improved form under floodlights that failed for 25 minutes during a first-half power cut. Mel Eves finally found a way through with this scrambled 50th minute goal but it wasn't quite enough to ensure progress. After four Euro campaigns in ten years, little could Wolves fans have imagined they would be waiting 27 seasons (and still counting!) for another.

Wolves at least managed League victories over Birmingham and Leeds in October, 1980, to lift their spirits in what already looked like becoming a drawn-out battle for survival and they kicked off November with another, this time at home to Sunderland. Wayne Clarke scored both goals in a 2-1 victory, this one from almost right on the line as John Richards also hovered in search of crumbs. But the empty seats in the new John Ireland Stand underlined the point that all was not well at the club.

For the second season running, Wolves enjoyed their visit to Old Trafford, when, having just beaten Sunderland and taken a good point on their visit to Tottenham, they held Manchester United to a 0-0 draw on November 12, 1980. Mick Hollifield, a young left-back born on Teesside, was having a decent run in the side as Derek Parkin came towards the end of his phenomenal Molineux career and is pictured chasing back here as Peter Daniel tangles with former Nottingham Forest striker Gary Birtles.

A brave save by Paul Bradshaw at the feet of the lunging Kenny Dalglish in Wolves' 1-0 defeat at Liverpool on December 20, 1980. The Molineux meeting of the clubs a month earlier had gone spectacularly the home side's way with even Emlyn Hughes scoring in a 4-1 win against his former club. But the veteran defender, seen behind Bradshaw here with Geoff Palmer at no 2, would play for the club only another five times as time caught up with him in his highly distinguished playing career.

When Wolves struggled in the League, they could often be relied on to produce a telling cup run and so it proved in 1980-81. After three straight Division One defeats, they drew 2-2 at Stoke to embark on an FA Cup adventure that started to take off with this 2-1 replay win three days later. Norman Bell and Hugh Atkinson watch Kenny Hibbitt lash in an equaliser that was followed by Mel Eves' winner.

Wolves made it five games unbeaten thanks to this 1-1 draw at Watford in the FA Cup fourth round on January 24, 1981. On the day Derek Parkin returned as substitute following a long absence, John Richards struck the visitors' goal and Andy Gray had his sights firmly on another with this shot.

Andy Gray again in the thick of the action in the FA Cup clash at Vicarage Road, the striker this time being denied by a somewhat unconvincing save by Watford keeper Steve Sherwood. Wolves were producing their best form in the FA Cup but, as against Stoke in the previous round, were taken to a replay by Graham Taylor's side. Gray netted an FA Cup final goal for Everton against Watford in 1984.

Derek Parkin was not a prolific scorer - ten goals in his club record 609 Wolves games prove that point - but he set his sights right with this shot that proved the decider in the 2-1 FA Cup replay victory at home to Watford on January 27, 1981. John Richards, on his way to finishing as the club's top scorer for the eighth and last time, had netted the side's first in front of a 30,854 crowd. Mel Eves is the no 11.

George Berry makes a fine challenge on Remi Moses to avert a moment of considerable danger in Wolves' home League derby against Albion on January 31, 1981. Paul Bradshaw and John McAlle - the latter in his final few months at Molineux - are the relieved duo as Bryan Robson and Cyrille Regis hover. Wolves found a way through the gloom to win 2-0 through Andy Gray and Mel Eves.

Norman Bell stepped off the subs' bench to become the man of the moment in this 3-1 home win over Wrexham in the fifth round of the FA Cup on February 14, 1981. Bell replaced Mel Eves and scored twice while John Richards netted once to keep the club's revival going. This was Wolves' ninth successive game unbeaten and their forward power was emphasised by the presence, too, of Wayne Clarke (left).

Wolves' League fortunes had turned round again by the time of this 1-0 home First Division defeat against Aston Villa on February 28, 1981 - a point underlined by the disallowing of this John Richards 'goal' despite Mel Eves' celebrations. Gordon Cowans, destined to move to Molineux 14 years later, is on the far left. Wolves had also lost at Ipswich the weekend but still had more Cup-fighting in them.

The sixth-round FA Cup draw sent Wolves on the long trip to Middlesbrough on March 7, 1981, and they shocked the 36,000 Ayresome Park crowd when John Richards stood aside and allowed Andy Gray space to send this seventh minute header (above) flashing past Billy Ashcroft and into the net. Boro came back to equalise but the 1-1 draw left Wolves well placed to reach their second FA Cup semi-final in three seasons, having pulled off another memorable League Cup triumph in between.

Molineux attracted its last 40,000-plus attendance three nights later in March, 1981, when Wolves finally ground down a Middlesbrough side who were managed by John Neal. Mel Eves, who was in a useful New Year goal-scoring run, dived full length here to break the ice in only the 11th minute, with John Richards up at his side in support. But any hopes that it would turn into a straightforward evening evaporated and Wolves were taken into 30 minutes of extra-time, with the score at 1-1.

Cometh the hour, cometh the man......just when Wolves needed some inspiration to break Middlesbrough down in their tense quarter-final replay, up popped John Richards (above) with a tidy finish that put the side in sight of a place in the last four. Jim Platt is the defeated keeper as Wolves restore their advantage.

Left: Boro and Wolves had each emphatically won their home game in that season's League meetings of the clubs but John Barnwell's men ensured they took the FA Cup bragging rights when substitute Norman Bell added a late third to find himself at the centre of some highly relieved celebrations.

For the second time in three years, there was FA Cup semi-final heartbreak for Wolves against London opposition. This time in 1980-81, it was Arsenal's rivals Tottenham who beat them, although this last-gasp Willie Carr penalty (above) salvaged a 2-2 draw when all seemed lost in the first game at Hillsborough. The spot-kick was controversially given for a challenge on Kenny Hibbitt by Glenn Hoddle, who curled in a free-kick for one of Spurs' goals. Hibbitt netted the first for John Barnwell's side. The replay at Arsenal four nights later was one-sided despite this attack (below) in which John Richards, Norman Bell and Mel Eves have their eyes on goal. Milija Aleksic is Spurs' keeper and Steve Perryman and Chris Hughton the men on the line. Tottenham beat Manchester City in the final, also via a replay.

# The Rot Sets In

Peter Daniel has to admit second best in this tussle with the imperious Alan Hansen but Wolves still pulled off a shock 1-0 home victory over Liverpool to launch the 1981-82 campaign in style. The Merseysiders, sunk by midfielder Mick Matthews' first goal in senior football, had just had a season off winning the League Championship but lifted the European Cup and League Cup by way of consolation! Wolves, having finished 18th the season before, failed to kick on from this win, losing four and drawing one of their next five matches.

Wolves lost nine of 16 games after beating Liverpool and won just three, although this 2-0 home win over Stoke on November 28, 1981, came in a brief revival. John Richards missed out from this opening but goals by Geoff Palmer and Mick Matthews saw Wolves home on a day when they kept their fifth straight League clean sheet. When fortunes dipped again, John Barnwell resigned on January 8, 1982. Mike England was an early contender as Jim Barron and Ian Ross became caretaker bosses but the club turned instead to Ian Greaves.

Hope for struggling Wolves on their visit to Anfield on January 16, 1982, as midfielder Hugh Atkinson toasts a goal in front of The Kop. Liverpool, at the height of their invincibility as they homed in on what was to be one of 11 titles they won in 18 years, hit back to triumph 2-1, though, to make light of these celebrations by Mick Matthews, Peter Daniel, Wayne Clarke and Andy Gray.

Wolves lurched into crisis by losing nine times in a row from the start of December and, by the time of this January 30 Molineux clash with Sunderland, feelings were running high, especially against chairman Harry Marshall. This game, in the middle of that damaging run, was a 1-0 defeat watched by a paltry 11,099 and the relegation die was very much cast by the 6-1 thrashing at Tottenham a fortnight later.

Temporary respite came with this 2-1 home win over Ipswich on February 27, 1982, in which Wayne Clarke, alongside John Richards, scored twice. Ex-England defender Mick Mills, later to team up in management for several years with Sammy Chung, is the defender. Clarke ended 1981-82 with six goals and the fact that that left him only one behind top scorers Andy Gray and Mel Eves said everything about the club's sorry season. As in the mid-1970s, they were relegated barely two years after lifting the League Cup.

Relegation duly came and Wolves were in a financial mess as well as one on the pitch. Doug Ellis (left) led a consortium that briefly took power in the summer of 1982 - one also including ex-Molineux keeper Malcolm Finlayson (second right). But any chance of stability for the likes of boss Ian Greaves (second left) and veteran midfielder Kenny Hibbitt disappeared when the club soon lapsed into Receivership.

Safe - just! John Richards looks on as Official Receiver Alistair Jones makes the historic announcement in July, 1982, that Wolves have avoided extinction by three minutes. In the middle is Assistant Receiver Alan Adam. The club would be chaired by long-time former Wolves striker Derek Dougan, who had returned to Molineux as part of the Bhatti regime, with Graham Hawkins as manager.

Derek Dougan, already a terrace idol at Wolves, addresses supporters on behalf of the new board at a mid-August meeting at Wolverhampton Civic Hall in 1982. The Bhattis would choose to keep the lowest of profiles in the game, even at Molineux, but Dougan's popularity was underlined by the size of this assembly. He was a brilliant public speaker and was warmly welcomed as chairman and chief executive. His long-time strike partner John Richards would, coincidentally, take on the job of Wolves MD a decade and a half later.

Despite the turmoil, pre-season training in 1982 contained all the usual banter, with Andy Gray at the heart of it as he ensured the cameras picked up on John Richards' holiday tan. Manager Graham Hawkins (right) and his no 2 Jim Barron, both on the Molineux playing staff in the 1960s, oversaw a fine start as Wolves stayed unbeaten in nine League games, the last eight of which brought clean sheets. Chairman and chief executive Derek Dougan stood on the terraces at the opening-day game at home to his former club Blackburn.

Wolves were top of Division Two by the time they recorded this 2-0 home win on September 25, 1982, over a Rotherham side who had Emlyn Hughes as player-manager. Right-back John Humphrey is the scorer about to get to his feet as Andy Gray stands over him, Wayne Clarke netting the other goal. This was Wolves' sixth successive clean sheet but they struggled for goals as the season progressed.

Wolves and Chelsea went up together in 1977. Six years later, the Londoners were on the fringe of the promotion race, their cause not helped by this 2-1 defeat at Molineux on January 22. Mel Eves is the no 10 celebrating a goal which prompted a less than enthusiastic response from Wayne Clarke! But the latter also scored on a day which brought Wolves their eighth victory in ten League games. Standing, hands on hips, is Colin Lee, then part of a Chelsea side who went up the following season. Left: Lee confronts Mel Eves at close quarters.

Below: Another important moment on the road to promotion as Mel Eves - set to finish top scorer with 19 goals - fires the equaliser in the home match with Carlisle on February 12, 1983. Wolves had lost their previous two games, one an FA Cup tie at Villa, but won 2-1 here, with substitute Billy Livingstone also on target. Alan Dodd is the man looking on while the player above Eves is Wolverhampton-born ex-Albion defender Dave Rushbury.

A star-studded opposition line-up as Wolves say farewell to the Second Division. Newcastle, resigned to another year outside the top flight despite the presence of no 7 Kevin Keegan, drew 2-2 at Molineux on May 14, 1983, Graham Hawkins' side having already won promotion against all the odds. Newcastle also had David McCreery (left), Chris Waddle and the leaping Terry McDermott in their side and would themselves go up 12 months later. The home trio on show are no 8 Billy Kellock, Mel Eves and John Pender.

Wolves had achieved promotion on a shoestring - and the loathed Bhatti regime unfortunately expected them to survive among the elite on the same basis. This 1-1 first-day home draw with Liverpool was about as good as it got, especially when Geoff Palmer opened the scoring from a penalty. Andy Gray flicks on here, with Liverpool no 6 Alan Hansen and midfield hard-man Graeme Souness - the latter linked in recent times with a takeover at Molineux - keeping a close eye on proceedings.

The rot set in firmly and quickly in 1982-83, with Wolves losing three matches in a row after drawing with Liverpool. A 1-1 home draw with Birmingham, secured by this header by Mel Eves that drew approving looks from John Pender and Alan Dodd, helped slightly, but five successive defeats followed in early autumn and the step-up in class was already proving to be beyond such a threadbare squad. John Richards had left by this time after scoring 194 goals in 486 games in a magnificent Molineux career.

John Burridge pounces to deny Ian Rush as Wolves come under pressure in their shock 1-0 First Division victory at Liverpool on January 14, 1984. Graham Hawkins' team had won only three times in the League all season, the first of them at Albion in late November, and remained bottom despite their first win at Anfield for 33 years. Success was sealed by an only goal for the club by Steve Mardenborough, who was in only because of an injury to Mel Eves. Rush, by contrast, already had 24 to his name that season. With Wolves failing to win away during their 2003-04 Premiership campaign, this Anfield clash remains Wolves' only top-flight away victory in over 23 years.

Relegation seemed inevitable for Wolves from the middle of the 1983-84 season and Graham Hawkins paid with his job in the spring. The club replaced him with Tommy Docherty but the Scot couldn't arrest the slide despite this Tony Evans goal which set up a 2-1 home victory over Crystal Palace on October 20, 1984. On-loan Jim Melrose, a success in his brief time at Molineux, netted the other but the fact the win ended a run of five successive Second Division defeats explains the pitiful 6,665 crowd.

A month after losing 3-1 to Huddersfield at Leeds Road in the League, Wolves were beaten by the same score there in a third-round FA Cup replay, the clubs having drawn 1-1 at Molineux. On a wintry night marked by an Alan Ainscow goal, Wolves' defeat was their eighth in ten matches, with the other two drawn. David Heywood (left) and John Humphrey are tested here by Mark Lillis' sprint.

Wolves fared as badly in the Second Division as they had in the First and finished bottom for the second successive season - the cue for Tommy Docherty to be replaced as manager by Sammy Chapman. Third Division life proved no easier, though, and it summed up how far the club had fallen that they were happy with home and away draws against neighbours Walsall in the League, although the Saddlers beat them in a two-leg League Cup tie. Above: no 11 Danny Crainie, substitute Campbell Chapman, Derek Ryan and Steve Stoutt watch as Mark Rees goes close in the goalless deadlock at Molineux on October 19, 1985. Below: Geoff Palmer, nearing the end of a Wolves career of 496 games, heads behind under pressure, much to the relief of Peter Zelem and Floyd Streete in the 1-1 Sunday morning draw at Fellows Park on February 9, when Micky Holmes scored for the visitors.

A goal for Dean Edwards at home to Third Division team of the season Reading on April 8, 1986. Wolves, having just won at Blackpool with an Edwards goal, went two up but lost 3-2 and continued their slide towards their third successive relegation. Reading won the title by seven points but had reason to remember a side managed by Sammy Chapman and, for a short autumn spell, by the returning Bill McGarry. It was Wolves who ended their historic run of 14 wins from the start of the season by drawing 2-2 at Elm Park in the October.

The Molineux that greeted Steve Bull in the 1986-87 Fourth Division campaign....a gate of 4,129 and Wolves losing, in this case 2-1 to Southend on December 20. The striker is pictured second right a week after he had scored his first League goal for the club in a victory in front of a 1,689 crowd at Hartlepool. There was no instant take-off for the club with Bull on board - Wolves lost five of the first six games after his signing. Also in shot are (from left) Steve Stoutt, no 2 Darren Oldroyd, Nicky Clarke and keeper Scott Barrett.

Following three years of virtually non-stop losing, Wolves did at least regain the winning habit in their first season in Division Four. On February 7, they embarked on a tremendous run of 15 victories in 19 games under Graham Turner to go within a fraction of automatic promotion. They narrowly missed out but had a second bite of the cherry through the play-off system introduced for the first time that year, only to surprisingly then run into problems against a side whom they had beaten home and away in the League and ended nine points ahead of.

Top: Aldershot goalkeeper Tony Lange, later to join Wolves, beats Steve Bull to a through ball in the visitors' 2-0 first-leg defeat at the Recreation Ground. It was only a third defeat in 22 games for a side who had beaten Colchester in the semi-final in the days before finals were played at Wembley.

Middle: Bull again in the thick of the action in the second leg against Aldershot, this time with a right-foot shot that fails to find the net. In front of a 19,962 turn-out - the biggest at Molineux for well over three years - Wolves lost 1-0 and so crashed 3-0 on aggregate.

Below: It was heartbreaking at the time to lose but the merest whiff of success had brought back some of the missing thousands, who would soon have much more to cheer as the sleeping giant stirred.

# The Stricken Giant Stirs

Left: Wolves' ex-Aston Villa youngster Phil Robinson is at full stretch in this challenge with Orient's Alan Comfort in the 2-0 home League win on December 19, 1987. On hand to help out is central defender Floyd Streete. The men from Molineux were top of Division Four and would stay there in a season that is remembered as the one a big club were reborn.

Below: Just champion! Party time is ahead for (from left) midfielder Phil Chard, Floyd Streete, Alistair Robertson and Robbie Dennison after Wolves beat Hartlepool 2-0 to make sure of winning the 1987-88 Division Four title. Turner's history-making side weren't satisfied yet, either...

Hand in hand with taking the Fourth Division by storm, Wolves were on a goal-laden run in the 1987-88 Sherpa Van Trophy, hammering Brentford and Peterborough 4-0 before overcoming John Barnwell's Notts County in the area final. Steve Bull ended the campaign with an amazing 52 goals, helped by this finish and another in the first half against the Magpies after also scoring in the 1-1 first-leg draw at Meadow Lane. Ex-Magpie Keith Downing scored as well in the second leg to set up a 3-0 win and some boisterous celebrations (below).

On to Wembley for the Sherpa Van Trophy final on May 29, 1988 - and a staggering 80,841 gate. The fact that Wolves' opponents were Burnley, another club steeped in tradition, clearly helped the occasion, which became a near-perfect one for Graham Turner's men as they won 2-0 with goals either side of half-time by Andy Mutch and Robbie Dennison. The trip to the twin towers came three weeks after Wolves' lifting of the Fourth Division title but they stayed on the boil sufficiently to make 1988 a double-winning year.

Above: Steve Bull, unusually absent from the list of goalscorers in Wolves' first appearance at the ground for eight years, bursts through Burnley's defence as strike partner Mutch, who used the day to net his 23rd goal of the season, strives to keep up with play.

Right: Robbie Dennison, a scorer with a terrific curling free-kick early in the second half, gives chase in the company of ex-Wolves midfielder Peter Daniel.

May 29, 1988, was the day the football world was reminded that Wolverhampton Wanderers were a big club - and these pictures underline the fact. Above: A section of the gold and black support at Wembley on an afternoon on which Wolves fans were estimated to have been responsible for up to 50,000 of the 80,841 attendance. Below: Celebration time again for players who became quite used to the adulation. Andy Thompson, flanked by substitute Jackie Gallagher, shows off the Sherpa Van Trophy while the non-playing Nicky Clarke (right) laps up the moment. Behind are Micky Holmes (in cap) and Steve Stoutt, who were given free transfers from Molineux a few days later.

Team spirit was at the hub of much of what Wolves achieved in the late 1980s as Graham Turner successfully gelled a collection of players with a hunger to show what they could do. The result was a tight-knit group who revelled in each other's company and who would graft endlessly for the common cause. Below: Home in triumph with the Sherpa Van Trophy as chairman Dick Homden gives a regal wave from the front of the bus while coach Barry Powell is a bit less restrained. On the right is long-serving physio Paul Darby.

After an opening-day defeat at Bury, Wolves found Third Division life as comfortable as in the Fourth and quickly confirmed themselves as 1988-89 promotion favourites. Four wins in five League games in September got them on the way, then they won eight in a row from mid-October to the end of November.

Above: An impressed Robbie Dennison sees Andy Mutch acrobatically score one of the goals that helped to secure the seventh of those wins - in a November 12 game with Huddersfield at Molineux. Floyd Streete and Steve Bull (2) also found the target. Bull and Mutch were to gain various international honours with England later that season as Wolves became the first club ever to win the titles of all four divisions.

Left: Robbie Dennison drives home during a mid-March home clash with Gillingham that turned into another goal-fest. Tim Steele was on the score-sheet in his first start for the club, the other goals in a 6-1 victory going to Andy Thompson, Steve Bull and Andy Mutch (2). Dennison played more than 350 games for the club from 1987 to 1997 and won 18 caps for Northern Ireland.

Floyd Streete (centre) and Alistair Robertson did much to help Mark Kendall keep a Wolves record number of clean sheets in 1987-88 - and they were still at it the following season. Here, they ensure the back door stays bolted in a 0-0 late-April draw at Huddersfield's Leeds Road in 1989. On the right is Welsh international midfielder Nigel Vaughan. Wolves beat Bristol City 2-0 at home two days later and became assured of promotion a few hours after that when Port Vale lost at home to Northampton.

Wolves still had four games to play when they confirmed a second successive promotion but the title remained up for grabs until the night Sheffield United arrived at Molineux on May 9, 1989. The Blades needed a point to go up, Wolves needed a point to become champions and Steve Bull needed one goal to make it 50 for the second consecutive season. All three targets were reached in a 2-2 draw in which Robbie Dennison completed the scoring with this brilliant free-kick early in the second half. Gary Bellamy and Nigel Vaughan look on.

Second Division life initially proved tough for Wolves, who were bottom of the table after the first five League games brought them three defeats and two draws. But the tide turned at Ipswich with a 3-1 win via goals by Andy Mutch (2) and Gary Bellamy, the latter of whom charges down David Lowe's shot here as Mark Venus (later of Ipswich), Mick Gooding and Shane Westley lend a hand.

Wolves produced an enterprising second-round Littlewoods League Cup performance at Graham Taylor's Aston Villa on September 20, 1989, only to slip to a first-leg 2-1 defeat when Stuart Gray - later to coach and serve as caretaker manager at Molineux - drove this shot (above) between Mark Venus and keeper Mark Kendall. Left: Gray is the man on the move again until Gary Bellamy, one of the unsung bargain buys in Graham Turner's admirable team, makes a telling tackle, much to the approval of the watching Nigel Vaughan. Andy Mutch scored at Villa Park for Wolves, who were held to a 1-1 draw in the return despite a brave headed equaliser by Steve Bull.

Wolves and Albion hadn't met since April, 1984, so the Hawthorns reunion on October 15, 1989, was big - especially for Wolves!

# Acquaintance renewed..

Above: Ex-Baggies man Robbie Dennison fires the first-half equaliser.

Right: Steve Bull lashes a dramatic last-gasp winner.

Below: At 1-1 deep in the second half, a penalty by Bernard McNally is well saved by Mark Kendall.

The joint efforts of Mark Kendall and Gary Bellamy repel a Leeds raid at Elland Road on October 21, 1989, but couldn't stop Wolves losing 1-0 to a club who won promotion the following spring and the First Division in 1992 in the last year before the Premiership was created. Kendall had soon regained his place from summer signing Tony Lange and would keep the jersey until being freed in the summer.

A hit and a miss for Steve Bull in Wolves' steady autumn progress in the Second Division. Left: The striker, with the first 130 of his club record 306 goals already to his credit, fires goalwards in the home game with Sheffield United in October, 1989, despite the presence of Paul Stancliffe - a defender who would shortly have a spell at Molineux. This effort missed the target in a 2-1 defeat but Bull was bang on (right) with the only goal of the game against West Ham a month later, much to the delight of Andy Mutch and new signing Paul Cook.

Is there something funny about me? Those two on the next table keep looking this way...what well-dressed Wolves mascots were wearing on early-1990s match-days. This was no ordinary trip, though, but the memorable exodus to Newcastle on a fleet of nine planes to witness the club's first match of the new decade. Steve Bull scored all the goals in Wolves' 4-1 victory to make the adventure a memorable one.

Albion were undone in a familiar way when they made the short hop to Molineux on March 20, 1990. Beaten by a late Steve Bull goal at The Hawthorns, they found themselves on the end of another 2-1 defeat, with the same striker again threading in a winner in the latter stages! Andy Mutch, as so often in the seven years of their alliance, is at his side on a night when Paul Cook was Wolves' other scorer.

# Levelling Out Again

Left: All action and all-out effort in Wolves' bid for an unlikely third promotion triumph in a row in the spring of 1990. The side had been on the fringes of the race for much of the season and the Molineux mood improved yet further with news that Sir Jack Hayward would be purchasing the club in the close season. Here, captain Gary Bellamy remains grounded while Paul Cook and Mark Venus do battle with Lee Chapman during Wolves' fine 1-0 home win over champions-to-be Leeds on March 31, 1990. Andy Mutch was the match-winner.

Below: Wolves ultimately fell short in their push for the play-offs and finished an unflattering tenth in the table following a last-day 4-0 hiding at West Ham. This 2-0 home win over Oxford a fortnight before the end of the campaign turned out to be the club's last victory of 1989-90 and, as usual, contained a goal by Steve Bull, who departed a month or so later to play for England in the World Cup finals in Italy.

Mike Stowell, signed permanently from Everton just over a year on from an impressive Molineux loan spell in 1988-89, saves bravely at the feet of Kevin Bartlett in Wolves' 1-1 League draw at Notts County on October 13, 1990. Towering above him are defenders Shane Westley (Wolves' scorer) and Gary Bellamy while substitute Paul Jones is the Wanderers man in the distance.

Paul Blades climbs high on the day Wolves surrendered their equal longest-ever unbeaten start to a League season. They went 12 Division Two games without losing - more than any club in any division that year - before slipping to a 2-0 defeat at Millwall in a Sunday TV game on October 25, 1992. The match was played on a waterlogged pitch at the old Den against a side containing Alex Rae and Paul Holsgrove, son of the former Wanderers defender John Holsgrove. Also in the photo are (from left) Steve Bull, Derek Mountfield, Paul Cook, Kevin Ashley and no 8 Jamie Moralee, who scored Millwall's second goal after the deadlock had been broken near the hour mark.

Derek Mountfield, an ex-Everton and Villa defender with a scoring knack, breaks the ice with a header in Wolves' 2-1 home win over Grimsby on November 28, 1992. Mark Burke was also on target in the club's third win in four games. In the background, the showpiece Billy Wright Stand is shown in its embryonic stages during an autumn in which fans were watching from a rebuilt North Bank (Stan Cullis Stand) for the first time since the mid-1980s. But on-field events were struggling to keep pace and Wolves finished a dismal 12th.

It had to be! On the day Wolves first opened the doors of the Billy Wright Stand - and gave debuts to Kevin Keen, no 10 David Kelly and the also-pictured Geoff Thomas as a sign of their vastly increased spending - Steve Bull scored the first goal. The striker turns away here after netting in the 3-1 home win over Bristol City on the first day of 1993-94 - a victory marred by Mark Venus' sending-off.

Graham Turner was under considerable pressure for his job as the 1993-94 season wore on but produced a final hurrah when his side impressively won 2-1 at Premiership club Ipswich in a fifth-round FA Cup replay on March 2. Lee Mills crashes in one of the goals here, Andy Thompson getting the other from a free-kick, as Wolves added to the scalps of Crystal Palace and Port Vale from earlier in the competition. In the quarter-final, they lost 1-0 at Chelsea, and Turner resigned three days later.

David Kelly shields the ball under pressure during Wolves' opening-day clash with Reading in August, 1994. Although Graham Taylor had been in charge for a month and a half at the end of the previous season, this was seen as the start of his era, with Steve Froggatt, Tony Daley and Neil Emblen signed over the summer. Wolves won 1-0 through a Froggatt goal but it was Mark McGhee's Reading, who included Adrian Williams, Scott Taylor, Mick Gooding, Simon Osborn and Michael Gilkes in their line-up, who impressed much more.

Above: After a draw at Notts County and an Anglo Italian Cup win at Lecce, Wolves beat Albion 2-0 in their second home game of 1994-95. The first goal came from Andy Thompson's penalty against his former club, then boyhood Baggies fan David Kelly added the killer blow with this second-half header that Neil Emblen watches in. There was sadness in the club, though, at news of the extent of Billy Wright's illness. He died within a week.

Wolves were big news in 1994-95, never more than when they faced Sheffield Wednesday - a strong Premiership side then - in the FA Cup, having won 3-2 at Mansfield in the third round. The draw sent them to Hillsborough, where Robbie Dennison gave another international winger, Chris Waddle, a run for his money (right) in a 0-0 draw marked by a dramatic 87th minute penalty save by Paul Jones from Chris Bart-Williams. That stop was a taste of what was to come in the replay. David Kelly's early goal was equalised by Mark Bright and the tie went to penalties in front of the live TV cameras. It was then Wolves provided a sensational story for the nation by recovering to win the shoot-out from 3-0 down, Jones saving from Bart-Williams (below) and later also from Waddle before Don Goodman smashed home the winning kick.

Having beaten one Mark McGhee team on the first day of 1994-95, Wolves defeated another when Premiership strugglers Leicester lost 1-0 on FA Cup fifth-round day at Molineux. Don Goodman was close with this header as he got ahead of Mike Whitlow and Simon Grayson but had the consolation of making the winner for ex-Leicester man David Kelly - a header voted Wolves' Goal of the Season.

David Kelly celebrates again, this time with Gordon Cowans as the goal-scoring toast. The midfielder is also congratulated by Don Goodman after sliding in the second-half equaliser in the 1-1 FA Cup sixth-round draw at another Premiership club, Crystal Palace. Wolves were undone by some spectacular Palace finishing in the replay and missed out on promotion as well by losing to Bolton in the play-off semi-final, their hopes undone by a mixture of erratic form and a cruel spate of long-term injuries to key players.

Hat-trick ecstasy for Iwan Roberts as he celebrates at The Hawthorns in Wolves' 4-2 win against Albion in September, 1996. Roberts was only a partial success after being signed by Mark McGhee that summer but also scored in the return in January. Steve Bull netted the other goal at Albion as Wolves took their place among the early promotion front-runners.

Right: Now it's the turn of Steve Bull! With this 76th minute decider on the visit to Manchester City in the autumn of 1996, Bull went past Albion's Tony Brown as the highest goalscorer of all time in West Midlands football. Bull, disappearing under a delirious group led by Jamie Smith and Mark Venus, with creator Robbie Dennison poised to join in, netted 23 times in a season in which Wolves lost out in the play-offs after finishing third.

Unconvincing as Wolves were in the League in 1997-98, a season in which they finished ninth in the table, they enjoyed their best FA Cup run for 17 years as they made it to the semi-finals by beating Darlington, Charlton, Wimbledon and Leeds. Unfortunately, they could go no further and lost 1-0 at Villa Park to the eventual double winners Arsenal. Elland Road quarter-final match-winner Don Goodman does battle here with Gunners left-back Nigel Winterburn, watched by Wolves defender Kevin Muscat.

Robbie Keane cuts loose in a 1-0 Division Two home win over Bury on September 26, 1998, that proved to be a landmark for his strike partner. Although the precocious teenager had already scored eight goals that season in the final weeks of the Mark McGhee reign, this particular day became more memorable for Steve Bull, whose diving header proved to be the last of his club record 306 Wolves goals.

Bizarre scenes in Wolves' 3-0 home win over Nottingham Forest on February 26, 2000, as keeper Dave Beasant - once a loan player at Molineux - loses his cool. He was enraged after kicking the ball away with the intention of allowing Lee Naylor (pictured in background) to receive treatment, only for Michael Branch to retrieve it and score to make it 3-0 just before half-time. Visiting boss David Platt called it the most remarkable 45 minutes he had ever known, a distressed Branch becoming one of three players substituted in a half in which three others, including Wolves top scorer Ade Akinbiyi, were sent off. Even Wolves manager Colin Lee was unhappy that the goal stood.

Wolves pushed hard for a play-off place in 1999-2000 in Colin Lee's first full season in charge, only to trail in seventh - the same fate that befell them 12 months earlier. Their last hopes of a top-six spot petered out with this 2-1 defeat against Bolton at the Reebok Stadium, where no 23 Ludovic Pollet had his sights on a second goal after netting earlier. With him are Steve Sedgley and Keith Curle.

# A Taste Of Gold

An entertaining side-show from Dean Sturridge as he punishes himself with a few press-ups after missing a sitter during Wolves' 4-1 win at relegation-bound Stockport on February 23, 2002. The striker scored twice at Edgeley Park in a victory that left the club five points clear at the top and seven clear of third place. But his 21 Wolves goals that season were still not enough to secure the seemingly inevitable promotion, Manchester City and Albion taking the top two spots and Dave Jones' side then missing out against Norwich in the play-offs.

Kenny Miller was red-hot during the 2002-03 promotion run-in, this finish in a 2-0 League victory at Preston on February 22 bringing him his ninth goal in seven matches and seeing him equal a post-war club record by netting in seven consecutive matches. Strike partner George Ndah was also highly prolific and broke the ice at Deepdale with a magnificent solo effort for his eighth goal in nine appearances.

Images of a fabulous day at the Millennium Stadium on Whit Monday, 2003. Above left: A section of the huge Wolves support - and a reminder of how long it had been since the club had last tasted top-flight football. Above right: Despite Wolves' 3-0 win over Sheffield United, keeper Matt Murray was named man of the match and deals superbly here with a cross, watched by two more former Academy products, Lee Naylor and Joleon Lescott. Below: Sir Jack Hayward and manager Dave Jones in happy embrace back at Molineux.

Above: The best moment in Wolves' Premiership season - and many other a season! Kenny Miller holds off a challenge from Mikael Silvestre and stylishly steers home the goal that despatched Sir Alex Ferguson's mighty Manchester United from Molineux on the end of a 1-0 defeat on January 17, 2004. The memorable win was followed by a worthy draw against Liverpool and Dave Jones' men fought hard before going down with Leeds and Leicester.

Left: Popular Wolves goalkeeper Matt Murray, who appeared in only one match in the club's Premiership campaign because of injury, receives the congratulations of Lee Naylor following yet another of his comebacks - this one in the FA Cup win at home to Championship rivals Millwall on January 8, 2005. By the time Murray preserved this clean sheet, Wolves had parted company with Dave Jones and installed Glenn Hoddle.

# Bright New Dawn

Above: A temporary change of roles for Joleon Lescott as he drives in the first goal in Wolves' exciting 4-2 victory over Sheffield United on the final day of the 2004-05 Championship season. The big defender had a fair knack for scoring and came up with 13 goals in 235 games for the club before departing for Everton in the close season of 2006 for around £5m. This win was witnessed by a 27,454 gate and was the club's 18th League game unbeaten. The run earned a final placing of ninth and carried Wolves into summer high in confidence - but the impetus was lost. The follow-up season was utterly miserable, so much so that it prompted the departure of Glenn Hoddle.

Left: Mick McCarthy was appointed as Hoddle's successor and was unveiled to the media only 12 days before the club's 2006-07 season kicked off with this 1-1 draw at Plymouth. Three days later came a standing ovation as a ten-man Wolves beat Ipswich at Molineux and, against all the odds, the side gradually put together a challenge for a play-off place. Before long, fans began to ask if MM did stand for Merlin the Magician, after all.

Joy for Wolves as they celebrate Jody Craddock's late headed equaliser in the 1-1 Championship draw at Birmingham in November, 2006. The side had followed up a fine win at Leeds by suffering five successive away defeats without scoring until they made the short trip for the Saturday lunchtime date at St Andrew's. The sequence looked like stretching to six until the central defender struck, to the obvious delight of (from left) Rob Edwards, Jemal Johnson, Seyi Olofinjana and ex-Blues centre-half Gary Breen.

More late derby fireworks from Wolves, this time in the Molineux clash with Albion on Sunday, March 11. Only seven minutes remained when substitute Jay Bothroyd picked up the ball, burst into space in the area and scored with a low left-foot shot that flashed beyond Baggies keeper Dean Kiely. It was a goal that stretched Wolves' tremendous run to six successive Championship victories and brought revenge over arch-rivals who had beaten them in the League at The Hawthorns and in the FA Cup at Molineux. No wonder Bothroyd was ecstatic - and Albion quartet Paul Robinson, Curtis Davies, Zoltan Gera and Neil Clement less so - after one of several spectacular finishes he came up with in 2006-07. Right: Goal-maker Stephen Ward was also thrilled by the breakthrough.

Gaffer's pride....Wolves manager Mick McCarthy hails the contribution of Neill Collins after the superb 4-1 victory over Leicester on the final afternoon of the regular 2006-07 Championship season. The success at the Walkers Stadium was the club's biggest of the campaign, booked a place in the play-offs and underlined the McCarthy era as an exciting new dawn.

# SCROLL OF HONOUR

**A**

Peter Abbott

Bob Adams

Luke Jacob Alexander

Geoff Allman

A Load Of Bull

Eric Asbury

Michael Ashmore

Sam James and Joe Astley

Colin Aston

Steve Aston

**B**

Ross Baker

Matt Bakewell

Peter Ball

Charlie Bamforth (in memory of "Jock" Bamforth)

Elizabeth Barker

Tom Barlow

Neil and Sheila Barnes

Peter Bartlett

John Bates

Leslie Bayliss

Anthony Bevington

Laurence Blackhall

Robert Blackhall

John Bleach

Hayden Lee Boden

Richard Boden

Nigel Bird Books

Roger Boot

Ian James Bourne

Patrick Bowen

Ulf Brennmo

Bryan Bridges

Gordon Brookes

Neil Mathew Broomfield

Dennis Joseph Bullas

David Paul Burrows

Andy Butt

**C**

Alfred Camilleri

Mick Canning

Don Carman

Peter Richard Carter and Family

John Clarke

Joseph Cleaver

David Cleveland

Ian Collett and David Collett

Chris Collier

Steve Conway

Craig Cooper

Clive Corbett

Richard Corcoran

Tony,Stephen,Robbie & Daniel Cowley

Steven Cox

Bob Crockett

John A Cross

George Cumming and James Black

**D**

Ken Dale

John Dallaway

Brian N Daniels

# SCROLL OF HONOUR

Harry Davenhill

Roy S Davies

The Davies Family

Kev Dawson

Paul Demaine

Brian and Helen Dennis

Benjamin Richard Disley

Darren Dixon

Philip Dodd

Keith and Shirley Dunn

Paul Wayne Dunne

**E**

Richard Ellam

Steve English

Christopher Michael Evans

Frazer Evans

George Evans

Walter Evans (Knucklas)

Matthew, George & Charlotte Everiss

**F**

Lynn Fancott

David Farmer

Roger D Fellows

Tim Fellows

Richard Frost

**G**

Dan Gaichas

Maurice Gelipter

Peter Gibb

F D Gilson (SLH)

John C Godfrey

John Godson

Tom Gosling

Mike Gough

Alan Campbell Grafton

Joseph Grant-Bicknell

Colin Gray

Andrew Green

John B Green

Robert H Green

Bill Griffiths

Peter and Wesley Griffiths

Robert Gubbins

Eileen Guest

**H**

Ross Habib

Alan Hall

Nigel Harcourt

Martin F Harold

Mrs K Harridence (in memory of)

Reg, Amy and Greg Harris

Daniel Harrison

Neil Harrison

Simon Harrison

Darren Hartle

Gil Hartle

Jim Heath

Bill Hickman

William John Hickman

Alwyn Hill

Rod Hill (Jersey)

Ken Holland

# SCROLL OF HONOUR

Phill Holmes

Barry Howarth

Jimmy Hughes

Sherrille Hyatt

**J**

Clive R Jones

Edward T Jones

Glen Jones

Graham Jones

Kenneth Jones

Kevin Jones

Stan Journeaux

**K**

David Keeling

Martin Kendrick

Brian Key

Andy Kidd

Joe King

**L**

Mark Lagram

John Lalley

Shawn and Pauline Law

William George Lawley

Rod Lawrence

Derek Reginald Lawton

Dave Leek

Raymond Lees

Andy Lewis

Tony Lewis

Andrew Light

Johann Lindenthal

Malcolm Lloyd

Rich, Hann and Will Lloyd

Ian Michael Long

David Lowe

Duncan Lowe

Nigel Lowe

Peter C Lowe

Barrie and Nina Lucas

**M**

Gwilym Machin

Tony Mallam

Craig Malone

Ian N Mason

Oliver Matthews

Conan Patrick McGuinness

John McIvor

Paddy McShane (Irish Wolves)

Jean-Pierre Micallef

Tarcisio Mifsud

Eric Millington

Paul, Matt and Owen Molloy

Andrew Moore

Dave Vernon Morris

Lee Evan Morris

Philip Kaye Morris

Kenneth Munk

Ron Myatt

**N**

Andrew Narraway

Geoffrey Narraway

Paul Narraway

# SCROLL OF HONOUR

Stephen Naylor

Frederick Nevard

Michael Newell

Mark Nicholls and Family

Warren and Dawn Nicholls (Canada)

**O**

Tony Oram

Keith Alexander Owen

**P**

Andrew Page

Gary Page

Barry and Alethea Parker

Keith Parkes

Stuart Parry

Matt and Tom Partridge

Ron and Shirley Peacock

Douglas John Pearl

Reg, Alan, Richard and Mark Pearse

David Phillips

Malcolm Phipps

Melvyn Colin Ponder

Robert Poulton

Paul (Octy), Steven, Charlotte Preece

Russell Price

Martyn Pritchard

Terence Prosser

Roy Pusey

**R**

Norman Edward Radford

Clifford Raison

Andrew Peter Raybould

Mike Redfern

Callum and Trevor Reed

Barry Rodgers

John Rowding

Chris Rowsell

Arthur and Jane Rudge

Patrick Rynn

**S**

Glen Saari

Jamie Sakalys

Chris Salmon

Arthur Edward Salusbury

Michael F Sampson

Mark Sawbridge

Peter J Schofield

Richard Sharples

Alan Shave

F Bernard Shaw

Ian Shepherd

Ken Sherwood

Max and Carys Sidbotham

Gemima Simpson

George Sinagra

Rod Skinner

Geoff/Dawn Smith

Matthew Paul Smith

Sara Smyth

Dave Snow

Jan W Sonderlo

Adrian Starkey

Eddie Starrs

# Scroll Of Honour

Ron Stevens

Andy Strange

**T**

Owen Tanner

Alan Frank Taylor

Jonathan L Taylor

Keith N Taylor

Hannah Ainsley Thomas

Roger Thomas

Jack Francis Tibbetts

John Edward Tilley

Jon Tomkins

Glyn Tunney and Emma Evans

Philip F Turner

Tony Turpin

**V**

Anil Varma

George Voulgaris

Petr "Prague Wolf" Voves

**W**

Eddie Walker

Tyrone Walsh

Simon Ashley Walters

Anthony Warrilow

Mark Watts

David A Weaver

Barrie C Webb

Steven Wells

Mike Westwood

Ken Westwood

Laurence Westwood

George and Greg Whelan

Bethany and Jazlin White

David Alan White (1941-2005)

Adam Whitehouse

Fred Whitehouse

Adrian Whitehurst

Dave Wilkins

Dave Williams

Joan and Peter Williams

Judith A Williams

Nick Williams

Steve Williams

Derek Andrew Wilson

Ian Windsor

Darren John Winwood

John Withers

David Wollam

Carl Wood

Kevin J Woodall

Andrew L M Wright

Michael Wright

Terry Wright

Tony Wright

**Y**

Barry Young

# Other Wolves titles by Thomas Publications

(All written by David Instone unless otherwise stated)

**The Bully Years (£8.99)**

**Wolves: Exclusive! (£6.99)**

**Sir Jack (£12.99)**

**Forever Wolves (£16.99)**

**Running With Wolves by Peter Lansley (£16.99)**

**Wolves: The Glory Years (£16.99)**

# Other titles by Thomas Publications

**When We Won the Cup (£15.99)**

**Le Tissier (£14.99)**

**Forever Villa (£17.99)**

**Forever Albion (£17.99)**

Thomas Publications are also co-sponsors of
**Wolverhampton Wanderers: The Official History,**
the stirring dvd which was produced by ILC Sport late in 2006

All these products are available by writing to:
Thomas Publications
PO Box 17
Newport
Shropshire
TF10 7WT

by phoning:
07734 440095

or by emailing:
info@thomaspublications.co.uk

**Further information about all of the above titles can be
obtained by logging on to our website:
www.thomaspublications.co.uk**